THE
SON
Who Chases the
FATHER

*"Resolving to be the man that God calls
out to and every child cries out for."*

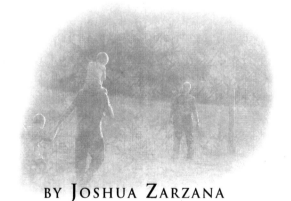

BY JOSHUA ZARZANA

TABLE OF CONTENTS

DEDICATED TO:

My dad, who helped teach me that the Father's
redeeming grace is the greatest treasure
any man can chase.

My brave and wonderful mother, whose silent prayers
helped rescue me from a lost
and meaningless life.

My wife, who has endured my years of maturing with
love and acceptance. You are a true woman of women.
Without your support, this book
never would have been accomplished.

My sons Christian and Alex, who show me every day
that love is open and genuine to the
man who desires it.

Special thanks to:

My biggest brother, Brandon Zarzana, and my
outstanding Uncle Tom Jenisch for taking time to help
in the grueling process of
proof reading this book.

My teacher and friend Dr. Val Clemen.

Your wisdom and insight is precious to me.
Thank you for taking time to read this work twice over
before giving your opinion.
Rest assured, I listened.

My editor Brian Smith. You are my true friend and
affectionate brother in Christ. Without major you editing
skil sets. This book wood be
have been not so grate.

Written for:

My God. I pray this message resonates Your glory to all
who read it. You are my deepest hope and
the best reason I have to smile. I love You.

PREFACE

The world is messed up. Corruption, greed, racism, jealousy, hatred... The list of problems is endless. And this book acknowledges the world's sad, sinful state.

But this book is about more than human failure. It's about the possibility of rising above our failures. Helen Keller said, "Though the world is full of suffering, it is full also of the overcoming of it." In this world, good *can* prevail. *But will it prevail?*

A little boy once wondered about the answer to this question, and he hoped to find his answer through his father, in whose life evil was prevailing. All the little boy knew was that he needed someone to look up to, someone to respect, someone to imitate. A hero. This book is that little boy's story. The little boy is me.

Will good prevail? We all provide part of the answer through our decisions and actions in our individual lives. This book is meant to inspire you to live and answer well.

This book is for:

Fathers. Among today's many societal problems, I count *fatherlessness* at or near the top of the list. Fatherlessness—whether the physical absence of a father or the emotional, negligent "absence" or even abuse of a father who is present in body—is an epidemic that is spreading at an accelerating rate. As a man who has now experienced what it is both to live as a son and to live as a father, I write to challenge and encourage you. No matter what odds are stacked against you, you don't have to contribute to the epidemic. Rather, you can become part of the remedy in a dark, hurting world.

Sons. No son can say that he had a perfect *earthly* father, but we have the opportunity to know a perfect *heavenly* Father. Regardless of what type of father you have on earth, you are meant to become a man who chases after your heavenly Father. We are to chase Him, so that we might become like Him. I tell this story to you in hopes of showing you just how badly we need God in our lives and how He can turn us into the men that we all hope to become.

Daughters. You are a gift from God. A treasured light loved by the Father. So many men have become so very lost in today's age. Yet these men are not without hope. I have come to know that your wisdom and life giving words have the potential to change and turn a lost man to God. I encourage you then, to become the loving mouth piece of God that every man needs. As you read, please consider the deep influence that your words and actions have upon the men who seek to answer the big questions about their world impact, about their identity. The Holy Spirit speaks in many ways. Does He speak through you?

Youth. We all know that this world is in big trouble. Where the world goes next very much depends on *you*—the decisions that you will make over the coming decades. As a generation, you—or *we,* if you'll accept a guy in his early thirties—have the potential of pulling the world down into a deeper and darker pit, or up toward a shining, glorious future. I am an optimist, and so I believe that this generation has the ability to turn things around. But I am a *realistic* optimist, and so I harbor no illusions about the length of the journey and the difficulty of the task ahead, if we are going to turn things around.

I write this book for you then, to help you consider the *inner* journey you must pursue in order to become an active, positive change agent in the world *outside* of you.

PLEASE READ THIS. You will notice the above picture that creates a short break(s) within each chapter. When you see this picture (or when you have finished the chapter), consider it your personal invitation to stop and visit *chasethefather.com*. I have created this website for a number of purposes. One purpose for the site, is to invite you the reader, to share your thoughts, insights and wisdom with other readers (including myself) about some of the topics you will come across. For instance, the topic of tragedy comes up in the book. There will be questions on the website like, "What are some ways that you think a person could best respond to tragedy? What are some Biblical examples of characters responding to tragedy in the right or wrong way? What personal tragedies have you been able to overcome in life? Are there any personal tragedies that you are still trying to overcome?" There are a number of questions like these that are presented on the website for each chapter. Your responses may be made public so that your wisdom can be shared with others. You will also have the opportunity to write your testimony, share stories of how God has personally used you, how God has used others to bless you, how this book has challenged you etc. It is my hope that you will join in and share your heart for the edification of others (Romans 14:12). I look forward to reading what you have to say and hope to get the chance to respond back. All my best to you, son or daughter, as you chase after the Father.

-Joshua Zarzana

Part I

A FATHER AND HIS SON

Chapter 1

A NIGHT NEVER FORGOTTEN

———～∾∾～———

It was a Friday night and my mom had just tucked me and my little brother into bed. As always, we said a prayer together before she walked out and gently closed the door behind her. I lay there in the dark, peacefully sinking into my warm and cozy bed, anticipating the boyhood pleasures of the next day. I'd wake up, enjoy breakfast, watch some Saturday morning cartoons, play some soccer outside with my three brothers and perhaps even visit with Dad while he worked in the garage. I fell asleep effortlessly in the calm night within a peaceful and secure home.

Next thing I knew, I was being shaken by the shoulder. "Wake up. Mom and Dad are fighting again," whispered my oldest brother, peering down at me. The fear on his face sobered me quickly to wakefulness. It was easy to see that something more urgent than my sleep was happening.

My little brother and I slid out of bed and followed our two older brothers to peer around the corner and down the hallway toward the kitchen. Thirty feet away we witnessed a child's worst fear coming to reality in our home. This was not the first time we had seen Mom and Dad fight, but never before had I felt my guts in the grip of this depth of fear. Both were yelling; neither was listening. My heart began to race as I watched them scream piercing words at one another.

I saw the fear on my brothers' faces, too. The four of us stood there silently, wondering what was happening. Could any of us step in and stop this catastrophe? I looked to my oldest brother, hoping he would do something. But in his eyes I saw that he was just as locked up in fear as I was. I remember praying, *God, please do something.*

But He didn't. Instead, a remote control flew across the kitchen, smashing into pieces.

"Get out!" my mom yelled.

In angry silence, Dad did as he was told. He walked toward the front door, never noticing his four boys peeking around the corner. In that moment, even from a distance, I could see his face. Anger was no stranger to that face, but this was anger that I could *feel.* Even at that young age I sensed that something inside Dad had broken.

Don't worry, I tried to convince myself. *He'll be back. Mom and Dad always make up.* But something in me couldn't escape the realization: This time was different.

I sought frantically for an answer. I wanted to chase my Dad into the night and scream at him, "Don't leave!" If I could send my present, more mature self back to that moment in time, I would have run after him and playfully wrestled him to the ground. It was a game he and I had often played at my young age. Maybe it would have disarmed the conflict. But my six-year-old feet didn't move. Just like the rest of my body, they were frozen from the shock and fear at what was happening.

I looked back to Mom. Though my mom is a slender woman, she sat down heavily at the kitchen table with a burdensome weight that would bear any chair down. She covered her face. Silent, broken, she wrestled internally with forces I couldn't comprehend. I wanted to go and hug her, but didn't know if it would help.

As I prepared myself to step toward her, my brother gently tugged on my shoulder, beckoning me back to bed. I turned towards my room and stumbled along in shock, wondering what would happen next. I silently crawled back into bed and pulled the cold sheets over my head. Once again, I tried to fall asleep, but my mind whirled. I no longer thought of Saturday morning cartoons or soccer. Feeling helpless, afraid and alone beneath my covers, I wondered if Dad would ever come back home or if Mom would ever be okay.

Everything Changes

I don't remember much detail of my life before or shortly after that event, but that one night is embedded firmly in my memory. I would love to tell you that this story ends with my mother and father getting back together. But I can't. Because it doesn't. This is a true story. And real life doesn't always have happy endings. And so it was that Dad never returned to be the man of the house, or the husband of my mom. After that night, there was only one person missing from the house. But even at the young age of six, I could easily recognize that more than just a person had vanished from the place I called home.

Here's one fact about fathers—*they are irreplaceable*. In a typical home, only the father gently wrestles his children to the ground. It is the father that the child looks up to, believing that nothing can hurt him, because Dad can overcome anything. It is commonly the father who sees his child take a spill and says, "Get back up. I know you are tougher than the tears." The role a father plays—the role a father is *meant* to play—is not that of an extra or a costar; to his children, he is the star.

When the father is gone, everything changes. A child is suddenly exposed, feeling weak, vulnerable, confused. The constancy of the perpetual, ever-since-birth togetherness of mom and dad is suddenly shattered. The child asks, "What comes next?" Sadly, no one has the answer the child wants—the answer the child needs. *When a marriage breaks, so also breaks the child's known world.* That is the harsh reality when a father and mother rend in two that which is supposed to remain one. Both parties become guilty of destroying the child's sense of peace and normalcy. And in most cases Dad walks away in shame, feeling like nothing more than a failure, another common reject.

I honestly wish I had chased after my dad into the night and perhaps stopped him from leaving. I think many children wonder, even in their later adult years, if they could have done something to keep Mom and Dad together. The days weren't too easy after Dad left. And I'm sure I'm not alone in this feeling. I am but one child who grew up without a father at home—one in a long and well-populated line of abandoned youth that extends back to creation and forward into the future.

Too many days passed before I recall Dad showing up again. The next clear memory I have of him is a night a couple of years later, on my eighth or ninth birthday. I remember how excited I was when Mom sat me down and told me Dad was coming to take me to Chuck E. Cheese. It wasn't just the fact that I was going to a place "where a kid can be a kid"; I was finally going to get some time with the man who was more valuable to me than any other man.

"He should be here any minute now, son," my mom said.

Upon hearing her words, I ran to the kitchen window and looked out into the night. I watched and waited for Dad's arrival with anticipation. Twenty minutes later I finally saw his headlights pull into the driveway. He was late but I didn't care. I grabbed my jacket and sailed out the front door. I relished my opportunity to occupy the front passenger seat, a privilege my older brothers made sure I seldom enjoyed. I hopped into the car and we left for our destination.

Dad owned a Chevrolet Beretta. It was black like the Knight Rider and had a moon roof through which you could look up into the shining night stars. It accelerated from zero to sixty with breathtaking quickness; Dad enjoyed demonstrating its capability. I felt like I was riding in the Batmobile with the hero himself.

Music blasted from the speakers. Dad was a fan of the oldies, which made me a fan of the oldies, too.

After traveling for about five minutes, Dad turned down the radio. "Josh, I want to take you somewhere before going to Chuck E. Cheese."

"Alright, Dad."

"I have someone very important that I want you to meet."

Twenty minutes later, on the other side of town, we pulled up to a house I had never seen before. Dad was suddenly acting strange. I remember him almost looking scared, but he was a proud man who never admitted fear. I followed behind him anxiously to the unfamiliar front door. I expected him to ring the doorbell, but he just walked in. We turned left and walked down a small, narrow hallway. I could hear a blow-dryer running in the bathroom ahead. Dad started calling out, "Honey? Honey?"

Wait a minute, I thought. *That's what Dad calls Mom. What's going on here?*

A happy-seeming woman with pale skin and curly, fire-red hair appeared from the bathroom.

Dad gestured toward me and said to her, "This is my son Josh."

She smiled and stretched out her hand. "It's nice to meet you, Josh."

I shook her hand. I can honestly say that I liked her from the moment I met her. I still didn't understand who she was though. She asked me a few questions about what kinds of things I liked. I answered her questions happily, thinking she was asking in order to give me something nice for my birthday.

After ten minutes of talk, though, I left empty-handed. Dad and I hopped back into the car to head to Chuck E. Cheese. Silence ensued, before Dad spoke up.

"Josh, do you know who you just met?"

"Not really, Dad."

"I'm sorry, Josh. I've never had the time to sit down and tell you this, but I'm not coming back home." He paused. "That woman you just met is very special to me, and I am planning to marry her."

"Okay, Dad."

What else could I say? What could a preadolescent boy say in response to his father's promise to abandon his family? If I had been older, I suppose I might have demanded, "What in the hell do you mean, you're marrying someone else?" But all I said was, "Okay, Dad."

The rest of the trip to Chuck E. Cheese was mostly silent. Once there, Dad and I had fun eating pizza and playing Skee Ball together. But later that night, after Dad had taken me back to the house and family he had abandoned, I was left with no distractions to take my mind off the now-confirmed truth: Dad was never coming back home.

Whom Does Tragedy Birth?

By a broken dream—of a boy losing his father—did much sorrow in my life come to be birthed in my youth. My unwelcome companions have been depression, insecurity, loneliness and many other brands of pain that I could not even now identify.

There's no way to accurately measure just how much a child—or the man or woman the child becomes—loses, perhaps never to be gained, when a father steps out of his intended role.

Tragedy in its ugliness takes many different forms. Mine was separated parents. Everyone who lives past a certain age will experience his or her own version of tragic trial or challenge, along with the despair it engenders. Perhaps you have already beheld deep tragedy, the kind that has considerably defined who you are now. We have no final say regarding the type or timing of our tragedy. It's inevitable, even for those who have lived the best of lives. Even if one looks back on decades of sheer joy, death of loved ones will eventually intrude. Wouldn't it be great if death and tragedy never existed? But a long time ago, in a land of paradise now vanished, sin was chosen over obedience, and human creation has been living with pain and despair ever since.

Tragedy is thus unavoidable in a world filled with sin and corruption. The story of humanity is a story of anguish. With all of the sorrow that history has seen, it's a wonder how joy still survives today. But even in the midst of our despairs, each of us can make a choice—not necessarily a choice of circumstances, but a choice of our response to them. *In tragedy, each of us makes a choice to either become broken down in defeat, or to be built up as a victor who holds strong to the concept of hope.*

Let me tell you about one example of a man who made the latter, victorious choice: He married his love in 1880. Though he had heart problems and was advised to live a life of simplicity and ease behind a desk, he chose to engage in strenuous activity, recognizing that through great effort comes great accomplishment.

He was successful, was respected and likely enjoyed life. He had been groomed for success, prepared for great things. Yet there came a day that shook him to his roots. He lost his young wife to kidney failure two days after she bore their daughter. They benefited from no warning symptoms; she was simply removed from his life. Within the next eleven hours, the man's sorrows deepened yet further as his mother died of typhoid fever. Within one day the man had lost two significant women in his life. His journal entry for that day was one large X and the sentence, "The light has gone out from my life."

Such tragedy would unrecoverably break many men. How many human souls have reached a limit to their anguish and given up? As Scripture testifies, "A man's spirit will endure sickness, but a crushed spirit who can bear?" (Proverbs 18:14). I have heard of men who have committed suicide for much less than what happened to this young man. But as I said before, a man can either take a tragedy and be broken by it in defeat or accept the tragedy and allow it over time to build him up as a victor, a role model or perhaps even into a man of God—the type of man who can change the world for the better.

Every man likely knows, in some respects, who it is that he wants to be. A man knows that he is meant to be courageous, a defender of justice. Perhaps that is why many boys want to become police officers. A man knows that he is supposed to be able to rise above his fears, and be willing to charge into danger for the sake of another. Perhaps that is why so many boys want to be firefighters. A man knows that life is supposed to be adventurous and is drawn inexorably into the unknown. Perhaps that is why so many boys want to become astronauts. A man knows that life is supposed to be fun, seasoned with joy and accomplishment. Perhaps that is why many boys want to be professional athletes.

There is something inside the heart of a boy that lingers on in manhood. There is a dream that never dies, a hope that embers on, aspiring to flame alive once more; even in brokenness.

As for the man who was born in 1880 that lost his wife and mother, history proclaims that he chose to rise a victor. This man, Theodore Roosevelt, went on to become one of the finest presidents America has ever known. He is remembered for living a life of historic proportions and leaving mankind with quotes like:

"The boy who is going to make a great man must not make up his mind merely to overcome a thousand obstacles, but to win in spite of a thousand repulses and defeats."

and

"A thorough knowledge of the Bible is worth more than a college education."

and

"The one thing I want to leave my children is an honorable name."

and

"To educate a man in mind and not in morals is to educate a menace to society."

and

"There has never yet been a man in our history who led a life of ease whose name is worth remembering."

These words resonate with nobility and character of the highest caliber. They testify to a man who rose above tragedy. Such victors are rare. Far more common are those who allow loss—or even just a normal life challenge—to build around them a prison of sorrow and defeat.

I am guilty of having made such a passive, defeatist decision. I blamed much of my sorrow and depression in my young years on my mom, who in truth did nothing but give of herself sacrificially to her family. I wanted something or someone to blame; it didn't occur to me that I could ever rise above the problem. Maybe you also have experienced life's pain—and maybe someone else really was to blame for it—but rather than assuming the responsibility to grow through and past it, you've wallowed as I did in self-pity, slinging mud at others.

How we respond to tragedy, then, makes all the difference in our own experience and in the experience of many whose lives we touch. This is the lesson that Roosevelt teaches. Quite simply, every individual must choose for themselves who they want to become, and by which of two mechanisms—one destructive, one constructive— will allow tragedy to define their life in a broken world. *Tragedy is sure to come, but what is birthed out of that tragedy is up to the one who bears it.*

Chapter 2

GOD IN THE RAIN

———

J ust as my home had been broken, so too was any comprehension of my having a relationship with God.

I grew up in a home with little order or discipline. Throughout one summer in particular, my oldest brother threw a party every Friday night while my mom was away at work. The popular kids swarmed our house, many of them about six years older than I. I looked up to them. I tried to be the funny kid, in hopes that they'd like and accept me. From my perspective, it seemed that drugs and alcohol were the common bond that all the cool kids shared. The prevalent logic for seeking popularity seemed to be: The drunker you got, the sillier you got; the sillier you got, the more people liked you.

How badly I wanted that acceptance. I could honestly say that I was willing to do almost anything for acceptance. I decided one night to try a few drinks and see what good feelings might come out of it. I acquired a forty-ounce container of vodka and headed over to a buddy's house. This was my night; I was going to get drunk and find acceptance at a new level with my friends.

We drank, a good four ounces each. Being a lightweight, I started to feel a buzz quickly. I was having a great time.

We played a few rounds of foosball, then one of my buddies asked, "What do you want to do next?"

"I don't know," I said. "What do you want to do?"

"Know of any good parties around here?"

"Nope."

"I know, let's go over to Amy's." (She was one of the popular, pretty girls who always knew what was going on.)

"Sounds good."

We made our way into the night—three tipsy teenagers up to no good—talking it up and enjoying the moment. We had walked a few blocks before encountering a small group of people hanging out by their car, chatting. One of them stood out to me because he wore a long black trench coat. I mean, really, who in the mid-1990s wore a black trench coat in the summer? Little did I know that he was about to play the role of a hero in my life.

I looked at this guy; he looked back at me. As we stared at each other for a moment, I felt like he was looking *into* me and could see what was really inside—a lost boy, out for a night on the town, looking for acceptance in all the wrong places. I turned my head away from Trench Coat Man and his friends and had walked ten yards past them. But then a voice shouted out, "Hey, guys, wait up!"

We turned around to see Trench Coat Man walking toward us. What did he want? We were minding our own business, on a mission, just looking for a party to hit.

"What are you guys up to tonight?" he asked.

"Not much," we answered.

We stood there awkwardly for several seconds, looking at each other. I'm pretty sure he smelled the alcohol on our breath.

"I know this is kind of weird." He shrugged, then continued. "But I felt that I needed to just tell you guys that God loves you."

Trench Coat Man was an anomaly in my experience, a first-ever. He was about the age of my older brother and his friends—the ones I looked up to—but here he was making mention of God. I'd never met anyone like this in my life; I didn't know such people existed. I figured every young person was out doing the same thing I was, getting high or drunk, living for the moment, avoiding parents, avoiding religion. Avoiding God.

"Thanks, man," one of my friends finally answered. "I appreciate hearing that."

I think he was genuine when he said it. And that about summed up our conversation. We turned around and continued walking in our original direction.

But I started thinking to myself. *God loves me?* It was a notion completely foreign to me, one that I'd never heard before—or at least never taken seriously. I knew that what I was doing was wrong, but I figured nobody really cared much.

A drop of rain on the back of my neck. *That's strange. Rain in the middle of the summer?* Well, actually it wasn't such a strange thing in the Pacific Northwest. But it had started out as a clear night with, I thought, zero chance of precipitation. Oddly, when that raindrop hit me, something started to go off inside me. *Why is it raining right now?*

It was as though I suddenly felt one of God's tears fall on me in sorrow.

My friends continued, but I stopped walking. I held my hand out to feel another single drop of rain. As I stood and looked down on that drop my friends turned around.

"What's up, Josh?"

"I think I'm freaking out, guys."

The rain started to fall a little harder.

"What do you mean?"

"I feel like God's tears are falling on me."

"Are you serious?"

"Yeah. I think I have to go."

"Come on and party with us."

"No, not tonight. Sorry, guys."

I turned around and started walking the other direction, hardly believing what was going on inside me. My friends didn't stop me. They probably watched me walk away, but I wouldn't know; I didn't bother looking back.

I didn't "find God" that night, but it was a defining moment. It was the first time I ever truly felt something supernatural.

Looking for a Sign on Highway 14

Though I had a raindrop fall upon me that felt like the love of God, I still had little interest in Him. I was shallow, like most fifteen-year-old boys, focused primarily on the young female body, video games and the occasional, ritualistic sporting activity with friends. I seriously doubted God's existence. Growing up in what felt like a legalistic church can do that to a boy. I remember the judgmental glances I received when I wore my torn and tattered jeans to church. But Mom always made sure I was there, especially when I didn't want to be. She didn't know what was going on inside me. At least, I don't think she did. This thing, this place they called a church, was for me torture to be endured. It fostered frustration and despair, not comfort, in my young heart and mind. I always felt out of place there.

I felt out of place everywhere.

To try and forget my pain during my high school years, I often went out on late-night runs through my neighborhood. I would settle into a rhythm and watch my shadow compress and lengthen beneath the soft street light. If I focused on that shadow enough, if I concentrated on something other than my sorrow, maybe that sorrow would vanish for a moment. Sometimes a tear would fall with the sweat as I ran. I fantasized lazily about someone—anyone; I wasn't picky—coming along and taking me away from this life I had grown to hate. That was my desire: that somehow everything would change. Things didn't change, though; they only got worse.

One night the depression and despair overwhelmed me, and I weighed the option of ending it all. Mom didn't know;

neither did my brothers. That night I went out running with the intention of extinguishing my life. I ran to the small bridge near home that crossed over Highway 14, stopped in the middle, leaned over the rail and took a good look down.

Maybe I should just end it all here, God.

I had no expectation of a response to my statement, but in that moment something amazing happened. I heard God in the back of my mind respond to me in a gentle yet powerful voice saying, *I have plans for you.*

I stood there for five minutes resting my hands on the cold steel, looking out from the overpass and watching the cars come and go beneath.

Tell me, what do I have worth living for?

I have plans for you. His line of reasoning wasn't complex.

I'm tired of the sadness, tired of living in this broken life.

I have plans for you.

I gave at least another five good reasons on why I no longer wanted to live. But I only heard those five words reiterated to me—*I have plans for you.* I should have been blown away by the fact that I heard anything at all, but I wasn't. Maybe I was too worn out by life to wonder. Even *if* God was speaking to me, I didn't want to hear Him; it seemed like too much hassle to believe in Him. And my depression and broken life made no sense to me if He did exist.

I kept up the dialog, though, aloud but in a whisper. "God, if You're real, I want You to prove Yourself to me."

What do you want?

My standard for proof wasn't very high. I just wanted some hope. I just wanted a day of joy and fun—what any kid wants.

"All I want is one day of sunshine and fun on beach day at camp." I was thinking of the Quaker camp I had gone to every year since I was eight.

After that I heard nothing but silence. I expected yet another response—a yes or a no at least but didn't get one. I walked off that bridge alive and expecting God, if He existed, to grant my request.

A Dark Storm, a Divine Comfort

Beach day at summer camp came a few weeks later. And, in honest truth, I had forgotten about my conversation with God on the overpass. It was a beautiful blue sunny day—not a cloud in sight. I thought nothing of the weather, though; I was too excited to see which girls would wear the most revealing swimwear. Out on the beach we played football and volleyball. The counselors brought out the grill to cook up hot dogs and burgers. It was a much-better-than-average day, but I can't say I actually felt happy. I played, but I didn't enjoy the games; I smiled, but I didn't laugh; I talked, but I found no significant pleasure in conversation. I felt mostly dead inside, even on a fabulous day of fun and bikinis. What more could a normal young boy ask for?

I forgot that I had already asked for more in asking God to prove Himself to me and He was about to remind me.

After forty-five minutes I heard someone behind me say, "Oh no, what is that?"

I turned around to see that it was my camp counselor who had spoken the worrisome words. He faced toward the ocean, so I naturally followed his gaze. One cloud, dark and ominous as I have never seen in my life, even to this day, was peeking its ugly head over the horizon. It was at this moment that my conversation with God on the bridge suddenly came flooding back into my mind, as though it had just happened.

"Maybe the storm will miss us," another counselor said. But the moment I saw that cloud, I knew that God had sent it for me. It wasn't going anywhere other than wherever I was. Within five minutes the blue sky had turned to black. The storm came rushing in from nowhere as if it were some screenwriter's sadistically ironic plot twist for a movie. The cloud shadowed the beach, took over the sky—no blue to be seen in any direction—and soon began pouring down a torrent of liquid despair accompanied by crashes of lightning. Everyone hurriedly packed up and started the mile-long hike back to the bus, but I stayed behind.

It was time for me to have it out with God.

Standing out on that beach alone I screamed into the storm, "One thing I asked of You, God!" The power from my voice was swept up effortlessly by the gusty winds, washed down and drowned by the rain. "One thing! And You can't even give me that!"

I would tell you in detail of what I said to God in that moment, but this book would quickly become one for mature audiences only. I no longer doubted God's existence as I tossed expletives and blasphemies into the storm. I was then—am now—convinced that nothing like that storm could have arisen the way it did unless it was conjured by a Higher Power. After cursing and screaming at God, one question stood out to me: "*Why* do you hate me God? Why do you hate me?"

This time no voice came to answer my question as it had on the bridge. In hearing only silence to my question, I left believing that God was out to get me. I assumed that God in His own vindictive way, didn't want me to enjoy even a single day. *He* didn't want me to experience a microgram of joy. *He* taunted me with the knowledge—His personal guarantee—that I would never receive anything I wanted. Angry with God, with life, at a level I'd never before experienced, I strode belligerently after the other campers to the bus, stomping nearly a mile through muddy puddles, mindless of the wet above and below.

My counselor spotted my face as I boarded. "You alright, Josh?"

I walked by him silently, sullenly, hoping he would leave me alone. He asked again, "You okay?"

I paused to make sure my I'm-fine mask was securely in place. "I'm fine."

"Maybe we can talk later?"

"Yeah, maybe." Whatever answer I needed, it wasn't going to come from my counselor.

Back at camp, everyone headed for the showers. I wanted to be alone, though, and held back. I went to the cafeteria and sat down with a cup of hot chocolate, with that question—*Why do You hate me, God?*—resonating through my head.

The others finished cleaning up, and I waited for all of them to leave the restroom before I took my shower. I undressed and stepped across the tiled threshold onto the shower floor. I turned on the water and adjusted the temperature. Then I pressed my head hard against the wall, letting the warm water hit my back.

Just white noise, like more rainfall. And meditation. Minutes pass.

"Why do You hate me, God?"

I can't say why it is that God decided to reveal Himself to me in that moment, but He did. And in a way that allowed no doubt: It was Him. I had asked that same question dozens of times in the preceding couple of hours. This would be the last time I would ever have to ask it. Though I did not see God in the shower with my eyes, I suddenly and unexpectedly felt an overwhelming presence of peace—*His peace*—come over me. It felt like a best friend had grabbed hold of me, was hugging me and was healing everything broken inside of me. I was overwhelmed by an enfolding force that I knew was not going to let go.

The words came out genuinely, "I'm sorry, God. I'm the one who has hated You." They were the truest words that had ever come from my lips.

It is impossible for me to fully explain with words what happened and what I felt in that moment. I just knew: This God I'd hated moments before was breaking me down, and causing me to fall in love with Him. *God is right here with me,* I thought, *and He sees my naked, ugly butt in the shower.*

I laughed. For the first time in years I laughed with honesty, from a spark of joy. And I could also feel God laughing with me. I was flooded by God's presence and His peace overwhelmed my soul. I had never felt so content and free from burden. It was the kind of moment about which people say, "I wish it would never end." I was changed in that moment. I had asked God for a beautiful sunny day. He didn't give me what I wanted; He gave me what I needed. And that's how I became a son who chases the Father.

In that moment, God reached out to me and I placed my hand in His. At first, I wondered who this God was that reached out to secure me in His grip. How could I know for sure? There are, after all, many religions with many gods. And so I searched, and in that search for the one true God I found that there is only one deity who relationally searches for the hearts of men. One God who stretched Himself out to give everything He could for His creation, so that they might know Him. One God who not only revealed Himself to mankind but lived with mankind. There is only one God like that, and you are only able to read about Him in the Bible. I am wholly convinced that that is the one God whom I met in the shower. And after meeting Him, everything inside me changed.

Everyone who knew me, knew me as a child of sorrow. But that was before I met God. After that event sometimes people would out-of-the-blue ask me why I was smiling. "I'm just happy," I would tell them. They obviously thought I was nuts; they would kind of stare at me and ponder my unsatisfying answer. But I couldn't give them any better answer than that: I was simply happy. Genuine, contented joy was one of the gifts that came to me when I first found God.

I am telling you this story for a reason. I tell it to let you know that God is in the rescue business. *God chases after the hearts of all, seeking those who will allow Him to repair, redeem and restore a broken life.* No soul on this earth is justified in saying, "God does not want me." For we are told that "the Lord is not slow to fulfill his promise as some count slowness, but is patient toward you, not wishing that any should perish, but that all should reach repentance" (2 Peter 3:9).

God wants you. He wants you to seek Him so that you might know Him. He wants you to come as you are with all of your sin and stain so that He can wash you clean. And He wants you to accept and believe in His love for you. God loves you and He reaches out to you even now as you read the pages of this book. He wants a relationship with you.

Is the feeling mutual?

Chapter 3

O FATHER, WHERE ART THOU?

———∾∾∾———

My life had been saved; I had found the one relationship that would remain constant, even in death.

But still, my world had its cracks and stains; it was still marred by brokenness. Mom was still gone a lot, working. The parties at home continued. And worst of all, Dad was still Dad.

Don't get me wrong, I know my dad loved me, even in my younger years; he just sucked at showing it. I recall one weekend in particular. Bacteria had somehow infected my jaw, and my face swelled up like the Elephant Man's. For about four days I had been taking amoxicillin—a creamy liquid mix that tasted like bubble gum—and the swelling had gone down. I know why the drug manufacturer made it taste so good, but in my case it was a big mistake. Man, did I love that stuff.

Dad came to pick up us four brothers for the weekend, and Mom carefully instructed him about how to administer the drug.

We arrived at his house and he took the amoxicillin out of my bag. "Come here, Josh."

"Yes, Dad."

"Do you know what to do with this?"

"Uh huh."

"Alright, then do it."

Dad handed me the pink liquid candy and left me to my own devices for the weekend. Big mistake number two.

I don't think an overdose of amoxicillin can kill you. To be honest, I'm not sure. If it could kill someone, I suppose it would have killed me that weekend. I was taking the proper dosage at the proper times, but I also swigged it as a between-meal snack. I was ingesting at least three times the prescribed amount. I started to notice a rash on my body—but nothing my shirt couldn't cover up.

It came time to head back to Mom's, and Dad asked for the amoxicillin back. He shook the empty bottle. "Where did it all go, son?"

"I took it. You know, like I'm supposed to?"

He looked confused. "Shouldn't there be some left?"

I smiled innocently. "Nope."

He didn't inquire any further—just left it at that. We got back home, and Mom was standing in the garage, excitedly awaiting our arrival. Dad unloaded his boys and was gone as quickly as he had come. Mom embraced each of us in turn. I loved it when she did that—waited for us outside, made us feel like we were wanted.

As Mom released me from my hug, something about me caught her attention. "What is that, Josh?"

"What, Mom?"

"Take off your shirt…"

I obeyed her command, and both she and I looked down upon my red-spotted torso.

"Oh my goodness," she intoned. "Josh, did your dad give you the amount of medicine he was supposed to?"

I spoke no words, but my eyes said everything. She grabbed the empty bottle out of my bag and her eyes got all big. She looked at the bottle. She aimed a piercing glare, not so much at me as through me. At last she spat out: "I'm going to kill him!"

My mom wasn't much one to make idle threats. I really don't know how the conversation went between my mom and dad concerning this issue. I suppose I would rather not think about it too much. After this incident, however, I had been awakened to a new truth. In some cases, Mom was better equipped to take proper care of her children than Dad was.

This was only one of many examples in the history of weekends under Dad's care when he failed at his fatherly duties. And some problems were bigger than empty medication bottles. A boy can only stay in denial for so long before realizing that his father isn't present, physically or emotionally, when his son needs him.

On this count, my younger brother, Jacob, was the most sensitive out of the four of us. He used to wear his feelings on his sleeve. If we made him happy, he would respond with love and affection. But when we made him mad—like when we called him by his nickname, "bacon bits" (don't ask me where it came from; it just stuck)—well, let's just say the repercussions could be dire.

After my older brothers, Matt and Brandon, were old enough to drive and weren't forced to visit Dad anymore, Jacob and I ended up the only ones going on those weekends. We spent time with our stepbrother playing games, and eating Hamburger Helper for dinner and pancakes for breakfast. I played chess with my stepmom, a weekend ritual that I always looked forward to. I think she sometimes let me win.

We enjoyed the time we spent at Dad's, but there was a problem. Dad was the main reason we were there, but many times he would be absent. Weekend after weekend he would have a band gig or something else going on that kept him from his kids. Jacob and I had both grown accustom to missing out on Dad when we visited, or so I thought, at least. A weekend eventually came along that challenged my assumption. Friday and Saturday came and went as normal, but when this particular Sunday came, Jacob and I were surprised to find Dad at home and ready to watch some morning cartoons with his boys. We sat down to breakfast together on the couch, eating pancakes covered in butter and syrup. Jacob was on Dad's left and I was on his right. His arms stretched across our shoulders in embrace as we laughed together at the hilarity of Garfield.

After enjoying a couple of cartoons together, Dad got up without a word and started walking toward the front door. I stayed in my seat but Jacob leaped up with an urgency I had never seen in him before, and he asked, "Where you going, Dad?" He didn't shout it, but I could see deep concern in the way he was standing.

"I have to go out and take care of some things today, son." He slung the words over his shoulder and continued toward the door.

"Can I come with you?"

"Not on this trip."

But in that moment, Dad saw that Jacob needed him. He turned around, knelt down on one knee to Jacob's eye level and said, "I promise that when I get home tonight, we will spend time together."

Jacob stood silently staring back at Dad. Even then, I recognized it as an important moment. We both hugged Dad, and he left.

That early evening when he got back, the man was exhausted. I don't know what he had done all day, but it seemed to have taken the life out of him. Jacob got all excited when he first heard Dad come through the door. No longer interested in finishing the game of Monopoly we had started, Jacob dashed out of the bedroom and ran to Dad in anticipation of spending the time that was promised at the start of the day. As I cleaned up the Monopoly game and began to head out of the room, Jacob came back in. I remember the look of deep disappointment on his face.

"What's up, Jake?"

"Dad just wants some time to relax before hanging out," he answered. "He said he'll come get us when he's ready."

When Dad said to wait, we listened. As much as we longed for his love, we also feared him. What that man said went, no questions asked. So we waited in the bedroom. Ten minutes passed, then fifteen. Jacob and I started to become anxious. Thirty minutes. I recall the look of hopelessness emerging on my little brother's face as each minute passed. Finally, I was done waiting. Fear of Dad or not, that man *would* spend time with us. I stood up and said, "I'm going to go check on Dad."

Jacob was silent. I walked to the living room where the TV was on. Dad was sitting in his armchair. Asleep.

I tiptoed closer to him and quietly stood a foot in front of him for a couple of minutes, wondering if I should wake him. I took the road that seemed the wiser and left him to his nap.

I returned to the bedroom and Jacob asked, "Can we come out now?"

I shook my head. "Dad's asleep, Jake."

"What?" He looked at me in dismay. I didn't answer his "What?" It wasn't a question, and I knew what he meant. "But he promised!" He stared dazedly through the doorway. "He promised."

Now, I said earlier that Jacob wore his feelings on his sleeve. The way he showed them was usually by taking action, rather than by showing emotion. But that night I watched my little brother break down for the first time. Sitting upright on the bed, he curled up and hid his face between his knees. I sat down next to him and thought about putting my arm around him. But sympathy wasn't my strong suit.

I watched my brother cry, not knowing what to do. In that moment I realized just how deep Jacob's love was for Dad. *It was a love that all fathers have a chance to receive and enjoy. But only some take the time to recognize it, to cherish it.*

Jacob cried for a good ten minutes, then finally forced back the tears. We played some more Monopoly without talking of anything but trades and good rolls.

After an hour, Jacob abruptly stood and walked from the room. I followed timidly and watched from the hallway. It was one of my brother's bravest moments in his young life. Dad was still sleeping, but Jacob stood in front of him and spoke up anyway.

"Dad, it's seven o'clock. Are you going to wake up now?"

Dad's eyes opened wide as though he had been brought back from the dead. "Seven o'clock!"

My brother stood watching him. I saw in my Dad's eyes that he recognized the wound he had inflicted on his boy. For the first time I could remember, Dad's face showed genuine remorse.

"I am so sorry, Jacob," he said with obvious regret.

Jake waited a moment, then said, "I forgive you, Dad."

I think that that night changed a part of my Dad. He had broken a solemn promise to his ten-year-old son, and he knew he could offer no excuse for not keeping his word. I was seeing something positive in him that I'd never seen before, but I was also old enough to wonder whether that something would last any length of time, or whether Dad would just let us down again next time. This was a good sign, but was it a sign of anything real and lasting?

Many sons have endured this same pain and greater. Too many sons. Every father is meant to carry and personally own a certain responsibility, to maintain a certain level of integrity, especially toward his family. But as surely as the world turns, every father makes his mistakes, piles on his regrets and before he knows it has lost touch with the greatest treasure of all: *Love*.

Here's a strange reality: The love of the children is still there; it's just that the father can disconnect from it. As a son, well acquainted with disappointment, I know one thing: In spite of all the mistakes, all the pain and wounds that Dad caused me through his poor decision making, I still loved him. I couldn't stop loving him; it is the natural affection hardwired into a son for his father.

Every father has the opportunity to venture into the love of his children. So then, why don't we see more fathers enjoying their children's love? *Because a father must first venture into his own soul before he can know the depth of love that is held for him within his children's souls.* This is the journey that my Father needed to take, but a journey that he feared.

How often does a man look at his face? I mean really look at it. They say the soul is in the eyes, and I think sometimes I have seen my own. Sometimes that level of self-penetration is disturbing. But it's this kind of introspection—taking a good hard look at one's self—that allows a man to consider not only who he is, but who he is meant to be. And it's that gap between *who I am now* and *who I'm meant to be* that frightens us, because overcoming the gap means humility and risk and change and work. Yet, the moment one begins to consider one's self with genuine, courageous honesty is, I think, among the most important moments in a person's life. For without self-examination, change can't happen; without change, maturity remains out of reach.

Chapter 4

CHASING VANITY

This life is a long road, or so it seems at times. I recall how slowly late December passed when I was young. Peeping under the Christmas tree with anticipation, wondering what was in each package—that was an old-time favorite. The two weeks before Christmas were torture. Waiting to open presents has always been contrary to my nature. One year I even sneaked a peek inside the gifts my brothers got me. One was Ninja Turtle Ooze in a Play-Doh-style can. Yahtzee! (Of course, my little brother, Jacob, caught me looking and, suddenly the self-appointed protector of justice, pureed the ooze in the garbage disposal, and it was never seen again. Tragic.)

Ever so slowly did life seem to move in my young age. I sometimes wish I could go back to that time, a time when life's leisurely pace should have made it easier to treasure the precious moments. But of course at that age I didn't have the maturity to recognize the value of a present moment; I wasted them by the millions. That is one of the greatest tragedies of life for some, I believe. Even in adulthood we can easily forget just how precious life truly is. We fail to recognize that even in the mundane moments of life a moment worth clutching on to may be nearer than we think. I know this is a flaw that is likely common to every human.

We can fail to see how precious it is to have dear friends near us until we must separate from them. We can falter in recognizing the blessing of holding our little children in our arms until they suddenly become too big to lift. We can lack an appreciation of our youth until old age presses in to our frail bodies. We lose out when we do not rejoice in our old age, possessing a knowledge that we are that much closer to heaven. There is much in this life that can be deemed as precious but we have to take the time to observe and identify those blessings.

It is human nature to get swept up and forget to appreciate the joys that we should reflect upon. This is one reason that we so deeply need wisdom, for only the wise can hope to value life's deep blessings. Some of us need a helpful nudge along the path of wisdom; some of us need a vigorous shove. It's probably safe to say that all of us, at one time or another, *need* that vigorous shove. We are stubborn creatures, prideful beyond any hope at times, willing protagonists for our soul-devouring enemy. I've encountered ample evidence that "there is a way that seems right to a man, but its end is the way to death" (Proverbs 16:25).

My father traveled the deadly road of vanity. It was a path that both created and led to destruction—created destruction in the lives of people around him, and would eventually lead to his own ultimate destruction if he refused to change course. But for him, the neglect of his family to chase after worldly wealth and fame seemed completely reasonable. The man could put on a show unlike any other I had ever seen. He performed flawless satirical impersonations of Elvis and Buddy Holly. He was comical, entertaining, handsome, respected and perhaps even envied. This road brought happiness for the moment, a feeling of purpose and accomplishment. But in the end it was both unreasoned and lacking an ultimate purpose, nothing more than a road to vanity. *Many men before him have followed this road, as will far too many men after him.* I'm amazed how often we play ourselves for the fool. How easily we indulge our cravings for respect, fame and fortune—all leading toward destination: Vanity. Yet how good those wasted moments taste…in the moment. How great they feel.

I recall the taste quite distinctly.

Kissing Life Goodbye

It was late in the summer just before my first year of high school. I remember the evening well. I had just finished a game of soccer with friends—one of many we'd enjoyed together. The sun was setting and I was heading home for dinner. Along the way lay a familiar playground in which I experienced the many wondrous joys of childhood—launching myself from the swings, the furious games of tag and hide 'n' go seek with my brothers, the many hiding places for both.

This time, though, something was different about the playground. Something majestic and exciting. Something dangerous. Sitting alone on the swing set was a teenage girl. Dinner could wait. Fate had produced an opportunity for me that I was not willing to pass up.

As I moved in closer I couldn't see her face yet, but her light brown hair reflected the setting sun, and her skin glowed in the magical evening light. As I approached her, I did my best to play it cool, but could already feel myself becoming a nervous wreck inside. I walked past her, careful not to startle her, and I wordlessly sat down in the next swing over. I was afraid that speaking might spook her off. I dared only glance out the corner of my eye, hoping to catch a glimpse of her face. Was she pretty? Would she look at me? Might we make the fateful connecting of eyes?

Yahtzee! She looked my way! Only then did I turn to face her fully.

She smiled—a beautiful smile that left me dazed. "Hi," she said. "I'm Rebecca."

"I'm in love," I imagined myself saying. But all that came out was, "Hi."

But that two-letter word was all I needed to burst the dam and release many more words in the long exchange that followed. She was the new girl in town—you know, exotic just because she's unknown, the kind of girl that you imagine comes from a faraway land, escaped from a dread castle.

Before we parted, I accomplished my objective: I got her phone number. Shortly later we worked out the friendship thing, and then I acquired what I was really looking for—the boyfriend-girlfriend status! This was my first experience playing the protector, the listener, the man; it was all new, exhilarating territory. As with all new territories, there's only one first time experiencing it. Of all a boy's firsts in life, this was a big one—a land of milk and honey, a gold mine.

After getting to know one another through friendly and flirtatious conversation, our communication changed gradually into pretty much one thing—kissing.

Kissing the girl is undoubtedly one of a young man's life's highlights—a moment to be treasured if ever there was one. From the perspective of a young boy, little else compares to embracing his girl with a kiss. It was a period of weeks before we started kissing. And then kiss we did. Sometimes Rebecca's mom would be off to Portland for work, and when Mom's away the boyfriend shows up to play. I was living the dream.

But here's the thing about the dream: Kissing, the teenage boy's ultimate quest—it got old. And, well, kissing isn't really as ultimate as things could have gone. I was too scared to let things go any further, thank God. As the kissing got old, so did Rebecca's feelings toward me. We dated for about six weeks before Rebecca instructed another guy to call me and communicate that she was through with our relationship. That same guy dated her next. And yes, I still remember his name. Tragic.

Just as kissing can get old for a boy and his treacherous ex-girlfriend, so too can any other treasured worldly thing or experience become old for a seasoned individual. These things in and of themselves can prove empty, futile…vain. When we limit ourselves only to earthly pursuits, we come to the end of life and find ourselves saying with the wisest of all men, "Vanity of vanities! All is vanity" (Ecclesiastes 1:2). If all we chase is earthly vanity, we will look back one day and see years and decades filled with empty, meaningless moments.

This world only has so much to offer. If we are seeking to date the world and embrace it with a kiss, we might as well kiss life goodbye. Earthly ecstasy only goes so far before it downgrades to pleasure, then becomes normal, regular, and finally boring. These pleasures we pursue so passionately, when we achieve them, tend to lose their luster; their shine wears off. They become vain, unappreciated things and when all is said and done, our souls end up feeling even more hollow for all the disappointed expectations. *We need to consider and weigh carefully what we believe in, what we chase after. We need to learn to see things for what they truly are. We need to be men who chase after that which retains its shine. Precious treasures that can not be seen in the world but can be felt in the spirit. Commodities that eternally satisfy the soul of man.*

I said earlier that time once waned slowly but such a time now seems to be only a fading memory. Those two weeks before Christmas now seem like two days. I'm no longer tortured over which gifts I will or will not get; rather, I'm stressing over how to afford the presents for my own little ones, who have taken my place. Tragic.

"Where does the time go?" Untold riches await the one who holds the answer to that question. Time is one thing that many wish they could slow down, or even reverse. Sadly, time appears to be accelerating as quickly as ever and I hear it's only going to get worse. Day by day, time marches on without apology and the moments we wish we could freeze and relish at our leisure seem to dissipate as quickly as a breath on a cold morning. Opportunities to appreciate life pass us by every day, unrecognized as such until they've taken up residence in irretrievable history—opportunities to live, laugh and love. Opportunities to seek forgiveness and grant forgiveness. Opportunities to seek life and give life.

You see, *life is undoubtedly a gift, but it is a gift that can easily pass us by unless we remain alertly on the watch for it.* We all live a life filled with opportunity to bless and be blessed. Every day, openings present themselves for us to become better in the next moment than in the moment prior and yet we let them pass us by. Tragic.

You should have noticed by now that I have used the word *tragic* a number of times in this chapter. And this is for a reason. It is to show that much of life can be tragic. Life is surrounded by tragedy. And perhaps the greatest tragedy of all things tragic is this: that we can forget that life is a constant search for that which matters most. We never realize that we are to seek out change that is delivered by an unchangeable God. We fail to consider our worth from Him who has infinite worth.

And at the end of our days we perish for we never learn to reach out to an imperishable God.

Some Men

Some men have trouble figuring things out. They're among the greatest and the weakest of men. Some are able to recognize what matters most and maybe grab hold of it for a little while. But often, even when a man has held truth in his grasp, he can easily let it slip through his fingers.

For a time, King Nebuchadnezzar held the greatest truth: that the Lord is indeed "God of gods and Lord of kings…a revealer of mysteries…Most High God" and the protector of His followers (Daniel 2:47; 3:26-29). But King Nebuchadnezzar attained everything his heart desired, and the vain promise of worldly wealth and power fooled him into saying, pridefully, "Is not this great Babylon, which I have built by my mighty power as a royal residence and for the glory of my majesty?" (Daniel 4:30). In short, "Look at what I have done by my power and for my glory."

Now, out of all the statements that men throughout history have wished they could take back, these words from Nebuchadnezzar rank right up near the top. In return for the king's boastful pride, God rightly humbled this mere man. Mr. Nebuchadnezzar "was driven from among men and ate grass like an ox, and his body was wet with the dew of heaven till his hair grew as long as eagles' feathers, and his nails were like birds' claws" (Daniel 4:33).

God made Nebuchadnezzar look on the outside like he really was on the inside—an insane beast that chased vanity. Only when *reason* returned to Nebuchadnezzar was he able to resume his kingdom and his former glory (Daniel 4:36).

The lesson is clear. Man cannot live in continued blessing until he learns to humbly recognize and thank God for the blessings he already enjoys. Until then, man in his pride lives like a beast, animalistically looking for the next object or achievement to consume in his vain attempt to satiate his insatiable appetite—a hunger that can only be satisfied by God. When man achieves this hopeless, helpless state, God still reaches out in rescue; it is when he is most helpless that man most readily recognizes his need for God.

What God did to Nebuchadnezzar seems pretty wild (so to speak). But how often have we behaved like the king did? What kingdoms have we built up in our lives, thinking ourselves their true sovereigns? What accomplishments have we boasted, believing that we alone achieved them? No one has a corner on foolishness. *We must apply reason to life, recognizing how much we will always have to learn from God, and the ways we will always depend on Him.* When we reasonably and humbly come before Him, He grants us more reason (wisdom) and endows all we chase after with an eternal reason (a lasting purpose).

Relationship of Rescue and Rest

I remember as a young man believing I had it all figured out, that there was nothing more to learn about life. But time progressed, and reality and experience taught me, as they teach many men, that much more than mere knowledge is needed. One of my favorite Scripture passages says, "Come to me, all who labor and are heavy laden, and I will give you rest. Take my yoke upon you, and learn from me, for I am gentle and lowly in heart, and you will find rest for your souls. For my yoke is easy, and my burden is light" (Matthew 11:28-30). Jesus invites us to take His yoke—the farming implement that fitted across a beast of burden's neck and allowed it to pull a plow or a load with its shoulders—and to enter His classroom.

There is much that we can learn *from Jesus,* the all-wise God-man; He knows more than any other what is worth chasing after on this earth. But we learn best when we are *in Jesus,* when we experience Him. The Greek word for "learn" in this passage is *manthano,* which means to learn intellectually from study and observation. Anyone can *study* and see that the life of Jesus is one worth imitating, but we have been given so much greater an opportunity than that. We are invited not only to live *like* Jesus through study, but to live *with* Jesus in our lives. We can believe on Him, commune with Him, depend on Him. He is the help we need to keep us from pride and vanity, the one who can help men like Nebuchadnezzar—men like you and me—restore reason in our lives. He is the peace and purpose that the vain man needs, in order to find a life of true satisfaction and meaning. I am fully convinced that no fulfillment can be found that is greater than that in Jesus Christ.

Some of us will be heroes in our lifetimes. All of us *need* a hero to rescue us, and that rescuer is Jesus. His touch and His love alone can deliver a man from the deepest trenches of fool-heartedness and death. Corrie Ten Boom said it well: "There is no pit so deep that His love is not deeper still." *God has gone to astounding lengths—He gave His Son!—and will continue to lovingly intervene in our lives in His effort to pull us out of hopelessness and into right relationship with Him.* The only thing He won't do is make our decision for us; He is, as C.S. Lewis termed Him, "a gentleman" that way.

When we *choose* to chase after God, we step off the road of vanity and walk a journey that will lead to an imperishable reward. God then gives reason to our spirits and imbues life with reason. He fills our moments with meaning and directs our opportunities toward eternity-impacting targets. We only have so many given minutes and seconds in this life to walk a road of either vain pursuit or glorious conquest. Which road will you choose?

Do you see now why it is key to submit our wills to God? Letting Him teach and lead us is the *only* way to build a life constructed of moments that hold eternal value. We are prone within our humanity to chase after vanity, which will perish with this life. Without God, we might as well count everything as vain. But with Him—*in* Him—we enjoy purpose, life and peace in everything He calls His children to do. Consider the great wisdom of the psalmist: "Unless the LORD builds the house, those who build it labor in vain" (Psalms 127:1).

Who's building your house?

Chapter 5

THE PRODIGAL FATHER

———

We can all look back on our lives and create a list of people who had the most significant influence on us, people who helped define who we are today. Of course, nearly everyone makes some kind of impact, but I'm speaking of those few who have, for good or for harm, dug deep into our hearts and planted memories that can never be fully uprooted. For me, one of those people is my father's second wife. So many times I remember her behaving calmly in the clutch, especially when my brothers and I did the dumbest things.

Like the time my stepbrother, my brother Jacob and I went on a criminal spree of epic proportions. Like every kid, we loved to eat candy. Hundred Grand bars were among my favorites. I remember Jacob always wanting the Laffy Taffys or Nerds. We lived in a community with three gas stations nearby, and for us boys they all shared one interesting commonality: a large collection of junk food. However, money was short that summer, so if we were to gain what we wanted, we had little choice but to take the immoral course. The research and planning stage for our heist was in-depth and extensive—an entire day. We strategically decided that one of us would distract the gas attendant with dumb questions like, "How much for a gallon of gas?" while the other two embarked on a thieving rampage. We plotted to hit all three gas stations, and as it turned out our approach was sadly successful.

In all we must have stolen about thirty dollars' worth of candy. We were able to stuff a backpack full with our plunder. Our criminal enterprise's first day was a huge success, or so it seemed as we headed home to examine our loot at greater leisure. We overflowed with anticipation as we hid away in my stepbrother's room and prepared to open the backpack of sugary treasures, but as happens surprisingly often to young and unskilled perpetrators, in stepped the unwelcome and unannounced parental authority to see what we were up to.

"Oh my," said my stepmother, "what do you guys have in the back pack?"

"Nothing at all, ma'am…"

My stepbrother leaned across the backpack on the floor, covering it with his body. It was a pathetic sight, the perfect picture of the obviously guilty boy who believes he can hide his lie, pleading, "Nothing to be seen here!" The first day of our criminal careers quickly became our last as the gavel of justice swiftly made its descent. The candy was discovered, and I was sure all hell was about to break loose. So I thought at least. Ever so calmly, though, my stepmom simply asked questions…without a hint of anger in her voice. Her disappointment was evident, but so was her deep maturity and control in the situation. I wouldn't have been surprised if she had spanked us, as Dad had done on occasion with effective results. (I happen to believe that spanking has a place in parenting, but it is never to be done in anger.) I also half-expected the more destructive approach that many parents use—the cutting, denigrating words that strike deep and can leave scars for life upon the heart of a young culprit.

Such was not the reaction from the woman I had come to respect and call friend. She sent us all back to the gas stations—yes, all three stations, of course, one after the other—and required us to return the candy with an apology. None of the managers chose to prosecute us for our crime, but our thievery did not go without consequence. That summer a sizable fraction of our youth was spent cleaning up the garage. We also learned how much work a garden requires, performing, among other tasks, the planting of green beans—the fruit of our effort serving only as further punishment: the eating of said green beans. Where other parents might take the easy way out, that woman loved us enough to choose discipline that would lastingly change us for the better. Her constant manifestation of patience, kindness and love will stick with me forever. She practiced this same kind of love with all people—and with none more than my Dad.

Sometimes it only takes one touch of love, *true love*, to change a man. The gift of true and honest love can be weighed as the greatest treasure on the earth. *True love is a gift that is incomprehensible to some, and immeasurable to all.* This love can awaken the spirit of a man, causing him to look deep into his own soul and question whether he is worthy, or how he might change to become worthy. I believe this was the species of love that my father received from his second wife. The question remained: How would he respond? Would he soften or harden?

I recall her once saying to him, "Dave, your kids love you. You need to spend more time with them."

There it was, plain and simple; out of love came the strongest truth he had likely heard in months, if not years. I watched to see what would come out of Dad. What emerged was a behemoth that has bested men throughout all ages. A great monster named Pride that coils its long, strong tentacles inexorably all up inside of us. Some beasts seem untamable, unstoppable. In many of us, pride is like the indomitable offspring from the union of the immovable object with the unstoppable force, making its dwelling place within the soul. Some will admit, "I know that beast; it has lived in me; it's a part of me."

We need to be rescued from ourselves. We can't perform that rescue on ourselves. No other man can do more than assist in it; each knows well his own subjugation to the same beast, his own failure at subduing the tyrannical force of pride. Or if not pride, then some other seemingly invincible monster—maybe love of money or desire for women. Every man plays host to some kind of inner brute that he knows, short of rescue, will take over. To fail is human; we all possess a nature that fights contrary to that which we know we should do. This tendency inside us, helped along by the world, has a way of spawning desires that overwhelm the conscience and the will. Even when we have the greatest of treasures in our lives—the life-giving love and presence of God—we can still be blinded by this unholy alliance of evil, blinded to the gifts that are right in front of us.

That woman, my stepmother, sacrificially loved my father, and time and again tried to grip him by the heart, shake him and wake him to the gravity of his poor choices.

She was uncommon. She was beautiful, in love with the Lord and in love with my dad. But a person can only go so far—never being heard and never really being loved—before she finally breaks down and dies within. She stayed married to my dad some seven or eight years, living in a broken relationship that she tried so desperately to restore. She even got the stubborn man going to church, and he liked it. But in the end the small changes in my dad weren't enough to sustain her endurance, not when he so desperately needed to make the big changes.

She eventually fell in love with someone else, and one of the greatest blessings ever given to my father walked out of his life, into the arms of another man. My father was deeply wounded, as though a knife had been plunged between his ribs, gouging his heart. Pride was so intricately interwoven with his heart that it was hard at first to know whether the wound would be fatal to the beast or to Dad, if either.

Some men, wounded this way, would stubbornly try pulling the knife out. Let the blood pour for a while—take a chance of dying—as long as they could do it their own way. Others would pretend to go on with life as usual, letting scar tissue form around the knife, but also allowing infection to fester, enraging the inner beast still further.

And some men might go to a doctor.

One Eighty

Remember earlier, when I wrote about the night I anticipated Dad coming to pick me up for my birthday? The anticipation was largely due to my dad's car and the way he drove it. The engine rumbled when he stomped on the gas. He did that a lot, especially going down hills that made my stomach levitate into my chest. I would have cruised with that man anywhere, anytime. Trouble was, that was about as far as our relationship went. In the haze of the music and the car rides was a man sitting next to me whom I called Dad, but who didn't always act like a dad. So many years I had lived around him, learning his ways, desiring to be with him and to be like him. I don't think he knows just how much I idolized him; perhaps no father fully understands his impact on his son. *Even if he failed, I too wanted to be the same type of man, even if it led inevitably to my own failure.* I was starving for a model to follow, and I would take whatever I could from the life of this most significant male in my life.

To me, on the outside, my father seemed consistently content, happy with life. I believed, as every small boy does, that dad was invincible and unaffected, no matter what came his way. My perception changed after Dad lost love for the second time. It was the first time that I had ever seen my dad overcome with guilt and sadness. I recall the weekends after she left; they were even emptier than they had been before. Dad's heart had been broken, and he did not know how to respond to such a loss. The next many weekends at Dad's were filled with silence. I somehow recognized that Dad was working some things out within himself. I'm sure the questions *why* and *how* were paramount in his mind, and ultimately, the answer was quite simple. *When a man bathes freely in the world and lets his spirit soak up its influence to the point of saturation, he can typically expect a life of brokenness and unfulfillment.* This was the truth my father was discovering in those lonely days.

The world never has held—never will hold—the answer a man needs in becoming the hero his wife and children need. Yes, it offers bandages and short-term fixes that promise restoration and repair. But the ultimate healing, strength, wisdom and love that a man genuinely needs come only from God, *the one who artfully crafted the innermost depths of man. The one who heals the heart and seals it with His hope. The one who understands, contrary to the world's "wisdom," that man will always be lost without Him.* Little did my father know that God had been chasing him for years (just as He's chasing after all of us). You see, my friend, in my opinion, God desires to have a relationship with anyone who would chance to know Him. He has given us the ability to either renounce Him in pride or submit to Him in humility.

This was the choice that my father faced. It was time once again to make a choice, just as he had had many chances to make this same choice before. *We all have these chances, perhaps in every moment of every day; it is just a matter of whether or not we can recognize the opportunities as such.* My father had always been busy chasing the dream. Yet here he was, empty in the end. It was in recognition of this emptiness—recognition of the vanity in all that the world offers—that my father surrendered himself to God. I don't know exactly how it went down. I don't think it involved any magic words or magic feelings, just a man with a simple heart and mind who recognized his need for God.

For so many years, my father had been chasing the treasures of the world. Now, in one supreme moment, he found treasure that outweighed them all: repentance, forgiveness and a relationship with his Father, who had always patiently borne with his mistakes, absorbed his rebuffs, finally to receive him into His fold.

More Than a Teacher

The first time Dad started talking about God, on one of my weekend visits, came as a surprise to me. We usually talked about Bruce Lee's kung fu movies, we talked about sporting activities (specifically those involving the Raiders), we even talked video games. But we never talked God. To be honest, one of the reasons I enjoyed going to Dad's was knowing that God would never come up. I counted on church, or maybe the school system—not Dad—to educate me on all things divine. After all, what does a common man know of God anyway? That's why college professors are around…to explain the Trinity and to discuss whether man truly has a free will. What are theologians for? They're already there, by the thousands, ready to explain the mysteries of God.

So why should Dad bother trying to make sense of such things when he hardly understands them himself?

This I've learned: Some important truths are meant to be communicated in a special way, and often it is only the father or the mother who can effectively pass them along. Most children have no other human who loves them more than their parents—no one else on whom a child depends more for truth and guidance. For those reasons alone, truth must be communicated by parents, with utmost care. Children look to parents in their search for the right and the wrong. Even when we don't know it, our children are watching on the sidelines. We joke with our children that we are always watching them, but as we examine such a statement, we quickly find that the same can be said of them toward us. Always watching, always learning—sometimes lessons that will never be unlearned.

The greatest lesson I ever learned from my father was one that he did not know he was teaching me. In all honesty, I didn't recognize it as a lesson at the time. But that's the way of sons with their fathers: Even when the son does not know it, a lesson can indeed be unknowingly learned. After Dad's second wife left him, and he made a decision to give over all that he had to God, both the good and the bad. He was moved by God to seek forgiveness from those he had offended. I don't know exactly who all he called or otherwise got in touch with, but I do know that he determined in his heart to talk to each of his boys one on one, starting with the oldest. We were use to only spending time with Dad every other weekend, but a clear sense of urgency was working in our father, and he started showing up for us on "unassigned" days. One by one, Dad took us with him in the car to talk.

When my day came, I remember it well. The sun was shining from a blue sky as we travelled to Battle Ground, Washington. I wondered why Battle Ground. It held very little for visitors, and even less that seemed important for Dad or me. But as we neared, I realized where we were going. The church. The Foursquare church that Dad used to attend with his second wife. I wondered, *Why would he come back here?* A lot of my father's sadness had been birthed out of this place.

You see, this church was once pastored by the man who fell in love with my stepmother. He chose to abandon his calling as a pastor and ran off with her. I never imagined we'd purposefully come back here. Who wants to come anywhere near a church with a reputation of having been pastored by a home wrecker? Or to the place where your wife had been wooed and stolen?

We sat in that parking lot silently for about five minutes before Dad finally spoke. "Josh, it's my fault. All the pain I am going through, and the pain you are feeling from this happening, it's because of me."

I remember staring directly at him as he talked. He didn't look at me; I think he was too ashamed to try. I remember the tears falling from his eyes as he talked about all the forgiveness he didn't deserve. It is a moment that I am still overwhelmed to look back on today. It was the moment when I realized that a true change was occurring in my father. He had said *sorry* many times before, but this *sorry* was filled with remorse and repentance. *It was the kind of sorry that inspires change in a man. And hope in a boy.*

"I know I don't deserve your forgiveness," my dad said. "And I may continue to mess up. But I want you to know that I'm going to do everything I can to get it right from this moment on. If you are ever willing to give me another chance to love you right, I won't take it for granted."

My dad was willing to let me consider whether or not I really wanted to forgive him. He gave me all the time in the world to forgive him, and I had built up a lot of bitterness and tension from his mistakes of all the years past. But when I saw the genuineness in him, I could do little but say the words: "I forgive you, Dad."

I remember that after the words came out and a little time passed, I felt a huge weight eased from me. It felt like a physical burden was literally lifted from my body. I couldn't see any chains, but somehow I knew that some kind of shackles had been loosed. Since that day, a new relationship, characterized by love and trust, has formed between my father and me. All the years of the broken past have been healed and forgotten. Since that day, a new loving respect has grown between us, a bond that many fathers and sons only dream of. My dad pondered and grieved and healed over a period of weeks and months, but somewhere in there was that one moment's decision where he stepped onto the path of life and eternity. That is all it takes sometimes, *just one simple step in the right direction, with a resolve to continue moving in that same direction for good.*

It was an amazing thing to be a part of, the experience of God's redemption between my father and me. It is definitely among the most significant "pinnacle moments" of my life. God's grace flooded in as though the Hoover Dam had broken, and it washed over a dry and desolate land. So much beauty has been birthed out of that moment, beauty that human language cannot fully describe, but that a seeker can experience if he persists. As fathers, we can assuredly count on this: We will at some point in time cause damage to our children. We must then ask ourselves what we should do about the damage we've caused. I hope in the end you will be able to seek forgiveness and allow God to do his redemptive work in your life.

You might even start today, in the decision of a moment.

Is It Ever Too Late?

That said, I'm not going to try and sugarcoat the message and tell you that you'll receive instant forgiveness from your children. The ones you've harmed may *never* forgive you. And while restoring and maintaining relationships with your children is important, it is not *the* most important. *The most critical arena of forgiveness and fellowship lies between you and God.* It is in Him and through Him alone that one can live a life of blessing, real blessing. Through God, a man is empowered to love on a deeper level, for when he looks upon the cross he understands true sacrifice.

In eternity past God made the choice to love, and on the cross He demonstrated His resolve to love unconditionally, regardless of the response—acceptance or rejection. Christ looked upon His creation and said, "You're worth dying for."

Similarly we fathers look upon our creations, our children, the ones whom God has entrusted to our rough and fallible hands, for us to love and protect. God is calling out each of us—after the example and by the transforming power of Jesus on the cross—to be the man who gives sacrificially, the man who offers himself for his family, no matter what the cost.

And don't kid yourself, the cost is great. Sometimes we make it too easy on ourselves, measuring ourselves by the world's standards. *But the world's standards are clearly failing our children.* Without question, we must become something more than what the world expects. We must set ourselves as fathers, to be the men who seek after God's expectation, for *it is through His expectation that our best can be realized.*

Chapter 6

BECOMING THE HERO

⎯⎯∞⎯⎯

After Dad's second wife left the church with the pastor, many other people ended up leaving the congregation as well. Many could not believe what had happened and refused ever to set foot there where such evil had occurred. No one had more reason to leave than my old man.

But my father had just done one of the hardest things in his life—he'd submitted willingly to God's will. This was hard for him, not only because of the emotional pain, but because his decision was so real. And it stuck. He was no longer willing to do anything but that to which God called him. For days and weeks, my dad asked God to release him from the church where he'd been so damaged. But every time he asked, Dad said he received a resounding *No!* from God. He was supposed to stick it out for some reason that God wasn't revealing yet. It was Dad's choice, though, whether or not he would follow God's will. He could have left, and I am sure that God would not have held too much against him had he walked away. But Dad was sure of God's guidance, and he chose to remain. Many of the people who also stayed were surprised and even inspired by his decision.

As hard as it might be, heroes do what Dad did. *Heroes stick it out and hold strong in the places they don't want to be, because they know that those are the places they are meant to be.*

The Difference a Hero Makes

Through that experience I came to see my dad as heroic in several respects. He was willing to sacrifice his own will to follow the will of his Father above. He eventually became the worship leader for that broken church, bereft of its pastor, and now today, even though Dad no longer fellowships there, the church is thriving, to this day bringing people into the grace of Jesus Christ. Who knows if that would have been the story had he left. He filled a critical need at a critical time, and had he not remained faithful to God's calling, the church might have died altogether.

The lessons that one learns in youth always leave their marks on our core and help shape who we become in the future. One of the greatest lessons I was learning from my dad was to be a man who chases after God. I'm grateful for the timing; I, a teenage boy, was struggling to comprehend what a real man is and does.

Day by day I watched my father transform from the villain that he had been for so many years, into the hero that I always believed him to be. I cannot express in words just how great the impact was in those days as I watched a once broken man of the world turn into a restored workman of God. *Children believe that some things can never be restored, unless the hero comes through to save the day.* To me, my father was that hero. He demonstrated that heroes still exist, that though there is great evil in the world, it can indeed be overcome through the power of God. As I watched Dad's transformation, my esteem for the world's power was being dismantled, while my view of God's power was being restored.

That is what a hero does. A hero brings restoration, brings hope. *This is one task assigned to every father, and when he fails, evil succeeds.* The political philosopher Edmund Burke wisely said, "All that is necessary for the triumph of evil is that good men do nothing." How badly we need the men of this world to do something. So many lost children who despair of hope. Our hearts must reach out to them, and it starts by choosing to reach out to God and seek out what it is that He has planned for each of us individually.

Planting a Seed for Healing

Some of a father's decisions have profound consequences upon their children. It was for a reason that my dad was the way he was before he met God. Dad is the broken product of a sad series of men who failed to love him. The men of my father's life succeeded in breaking down my father's precious spirit as a child. It is amazing the penalty children can pay for the mistakes or outright cruelty of their parents. Many a child, in response to the parents' hypocrisy and the resulting pain, screams with all his or her might, "I will never be like them!" Some children succeed at becoming someone else, but often I've seen them paradoxically inherit from their parents the very traits they abhor. A family tree can be corrupted at its core, filled with decay, sin and death, and the ugly, bitter fruit is borne by one generation after another, a heritage of horror. My father paid a deep penalty because of the damage done him by the men in his life. He is ultimately the one responsible for failing his family, but he learned his life lessons from a history of failing men. My father discovered that *men of failure commonly breed men of failure.*

Dad told me that the realization that his children might follow in his footsteps was like a brick in the face. The heritage handed down to my father could easily have defined his sons' futures. Though Dad had made himself right with God, he realized that all the years he'd spent messing up were years of failure and misbehavior that his young sons witnessed and would likely imitate. So much bad we saw, so much good we missed seeing. Before Dad's transformation we were never shown how to love a wife, how to raise spiritually and relationally healthy children, how to establish correct priorities in the maze of life. We four brothers were paying and would continue to pay a formidable price for Dad's mistakes, and he now woke up to the peril that his sons might walk the same path.

It was nine o'clock at night, but the time was irrelevant to him. Dad got in his car and drove to the home where we, his boys, had lived without him for so many years. He parked across the street from Mom's and our house. I don't know how long he sat there looking through the uncurtained windows for his children, perhaps wishing he could live once again on the other side of those panes, longing once again to participate in home life. As the reality dawned on him how much he had missed, he could have berated himself and allowed the enemy to consume him with feelings of failure. But in this moment, my father's head and heart were territory where the enemy was thoroughly unwelcome. He came with a purpose and mission that would not be thwarted.

Dad gripped the steering wheel and started to pray. *Father, don't let it happen. Don't let my boys follow the same path that I walked. Don't let my mistakes become their mistakes. Please redeem the years when I was so foolish, so that my boys can have a hope and a future in You.*

I believe that event, that prayer, was a defining moment for my brothers and me. It is a prayer that God has continued to answer with a yes to this day. You see, God hears every prayer, and in His wisdom He sometimes says *no* or *not now* or *not in the way you expect.* But some prayers He answers with a decisive *Yes!* Dad's prayer was one of those. On that night, I believe a new foundation was laid, a plot of fresh and fertile ground for my brothers and me to plant ourselves upon. Certainly we were still capable of growing up into men who lived out the same mistakes as our father. But Dad was seeking God's redemption for all of us, asking the Lord to renew all of our hearts, to purify the pollution and decay that had crept in from the old family tree, so that his sons might begin a new heritage that would bear pure, eternal fruit. I don't know how far back the line of failed men extended into the past from that night. But from that point on, I can confidently say that the generational curse has been broken. Don't get me wrong—neither my brothers nor I are by any means sinless. But by God's grace, each of us has remained faithful to his wife, his children and most importantly to God.

There was a power that came from my father's prayer that night—*a power that you are meant to ask God for on behalf of your children as well.*

We can easily see the pattern: Wrong choices lead toward death but right choices lead to an abundant outpouring of life on those we love. The husband and father who loves his wife and family, as God calls him to, holds countless riches. He then shares his spiritual wealth with his children, and they with theirs. In this way, an inheritance of blessing is poured out onto the future generations who are wise enough to walk in the same way. These riches count for so much more than any dollar price tag the world might slap on them. Earthly riches will one day vanish as the hopeless vanity that they are, and we will be left holding only the eternal gifts that God has given us. Now is the time to choose these precious gifts, to receive them from a heavenly Father who loves us.

We Believed

I am not sure if my brothers remember this day, but I surely do. I'd passed many a meaningless Sunday morning in church. You know how church can become just another common part of life, like going to work, or paying the bills. I believe church can only truly impact a person who is seeking God first. Some think they're supposed to change their lifestyle, or let church change them, before God will accept them. But seeking God has to come first. This is one of the ways my father became our hero. He had given his heart first and foremost to God, and then church could make a real difference in him.

We sat in church that Sunday morning, just as on so many previous Sundays. I honestly don't remember any of the particulars of the message—it had to do with forgiveness and surrender to God—but I do remember the impact it had on my dad. Time came for the altar call. That time when congregants are called out to stand and identify themselves to the world, to announce by their actions, *I have issues. I have a deeper need for God than the rest of you.* No man likes to go there. *What if people judge me?* he may object. Or, *Can't I just go to God privately, at the altar of my heart?* That would be a lot less embarrassing.

Of course, anyone can take that path. But sometimes God calls a man to do more. Sometimes God calls a man to stand tall with bravery and move forward, regardless of what the world may think of him. My father responded to that call on this particular Sunday morning. When he first stood, I thought he was heading for the bathroom. My dad was not one to respond to altar calls. I watched him move toward the aisle and make a left turn toward the altar. Then I knew. My head jerked back, my eyes widened in amazement.

As I watched my father walk down a path to spiritual renewal, my chest swelled, my heart beat ever so hard with pride. None of us boys had anticipated this strange, new development. None of us was accustomed to the path our father was now treading; neither was he. But his courageous action caused me to believe all the more that he genuinely wanted to change. Oh, how much I wanted that change!

As I watched him move toward the altar, it became a moment for me that seemed to move in slow motion.

Why don't you go up there with him? I heard the Holy Spirit's question resonate in my heart. It felt like fire suddenly filled me upon hearing the request. *Put your hand on him; help him believe.*

My heart felt like it was thumping out of my chest. I was no altar boy. I did not want to walk up there. But next thing I knew, I was following after my father, emboldened by his courage. The image as I walked down that aisle is sealed in my mind still today: my father kneeling and bending to the floor, fully prostrate before God, brawny arms stretched forward, strong hands clenched together in prayer. *This is the picture of a real man!*

I knelt down next to him and placed my hand on him. After thirty seconds another took a knee next to him. I looked up to see Brandon, my oldest brother, looking across Dad's bent back at me; we both knew something big was going down. Then came Matt and Jacob. Four sons, covering our father in love, declaring our faith in him, believing that this was a man seeking genuine, permanent change. We knelt there with our hero for as long as he needed and wrapped our arms around a man bold enough to lay his heart and his life before God.

Is anything keeping you from doing the same? Let it go, and lay yourself down before the altar of God.

The son who chases the father. The father who chases after God. This is the legacy that you must leave your children. Show them a man who puts God first and foremost in his life. It is chief of all lessons; by its fulfillment are we able to pursue and fulfill all other lessons of value.

Who was your favorite childhood superhero? The one with the power to destroy evil and champion justice? My favorite used to be Batman. But now I know that true heroes don't need to leap from skyscrapers and defeat injustice. They only need take a leap of faith and trust in God's justice. I still watch my dad today, pondering the kind of man that he is, the kind of man he is trying to become. No, fathers, you are not and you never will be perfect in this life. But don't let that keep you from chasing after a perfect God. *The future of your children depends upon it.*

Chapter 7

WHO AM I?

—◦◦◦—

"Josh, when I lean left, you lean left. When I lean right, you lean right." These were my father's instructions as he prepared to place me on the back of his Goldwing motorcycle.

I was around ten years old and had never ridden on a motorcycle before. I surveyed the monstrous two-wheeled vehicle with apprehension. Children have a tendency to get scared when travelling sixty-plus miles per hour with no seatbelts and no doors to keep them from falling out. I swallowed my fears, though, because Dad was inviting me to take a ride with him.

Dad picked me up and sat me down on the bike before hopping on in front of me. He turned the key. The rumble vibrated through my small frame. I wrapped my arms tightly around his waist as we journeyed toward our destination. Fear gripped me a few times as we traveled—sometimes at high speed—but I trusted my dad to take care of me. There were a number of curves and turns along the way. I synchronized my body's movement with his. He leaned left, I leaned left. He leaned right, I leaned right. I remember looking up at the sun through the trees as we rode down nature's corridor. We travelled about forty-five minutes to a serene campground. Upon arriving at our destination safely, I got off that bike feeling more like a man. It was one of the greatest moments of my life—one of my many rites of passage.

That day on that bike I trusted my father to take me on a scary journey in hopes of arriving at a destination of peace and tranquility.

Now here I was, several years older, a struggling and troubled teenager who hoped to journey once more with his father in hopes of finding my purpose in life.

My young life was one long identity crisis.

In soccer I was always the backup player who came in when the "stars" needed a rest. My male coach never thought I was good enough to start.

My male band instructor blamed me for our school placing second in a marching parade. I loved playing but I no longer felt worthy, so I quit.

I had a male tennis coach who liked to ask me, "Why is it always you, Zarzana?" I had no answer; I could only look at him with a numbed expression on my face.

My older brother Matt didn't help. He gave me the nickname "Dumma" for all the dumb things I said and did. I came to believe that his assessment of me was entirely accurate. I longed for a man to tell me it wasn't true, but none was there.

I was a devastated little boy seeking affirmation from men. But all the men in my life looked at me, it seemed, and saw only a sorry adolescent disappointment. I came to believe that I was nothing more than a failure, a reject, a waste of time. I received numerous tongue lashings from men who tried to push me out of apathy. I still remember looking into the eyes of men who pointed the finger at me and said, "You are never going to amount to anything." Maybe they hoped those words would challenge me to respond back with an I'll-prove-you-wrong attitude. But I was broken, conditioned to accept the cutting words as truth.

My life was in crisis. I knew that I was supposed to grow up and become a man, but I needed a leader. I needed a male figure to come and speak words of affirmation and confidence into my life. Words like, "You may be a boy now, but I have no doubt that you can be made a man." I knew that I needed a sensei, a man to affirm my masculinity. And who better than a man who was confident enough to fall down on his knees?

I was living with Mom, but I was coming to realize that I needed a man. And now that my dad had changed, I could finally say that I knew one personally. I *needed* him.

In my search for recovery from a ruinous childhood, I somehow knew that the transformation I'd seen my father go through was the same kind of transformation I needed. Before, Dad had been damaged, but now he was restored. Before, Dad was insecure, but now he was confident. Dad once walked aimlessly, but now he followed a clear direction. For Dad, the old problems were gone. But for me, the same problems were still staring me in the face.

I could have tried to deal with my insecurities by myself, but Dad told me that he wanted to make up for all his years of failure.

It was time to take Dad up on his offer.

Getting with the Hero

Mom did a great job raising me. A full description of my appreciation for all the ways she showed me love would be impossible. I am forever grateful for her many sacrifices. But no mom can be a dad. And only in that sense was my parenting incomplete.

Allow me to get controversial for a moment. I believe that a mother's love is…well…a mother's love. And a father's love is something entirely different. A father's love is not more important than a mother's love. But when a boy wants to become a man, a father's loving instruction will trump a mother's every time. I needed a male mentor. A man to come by my side and show a male perspective on how to treat women, how to relate with other men, how to live a godly life as a man.

So I went to my mom and told her that I was hoping I could move in with Dad. I assumed that she would respond, "Out of the question"; she cherished her children and loved having us in her home. But she too had seen the deep change in Dad's life and was wisely aware that I needed to make changes in mine. She knew that I needed a positive male figure.

I got my mom's approval but, even with her consent, I wondered how Dad would react to my idea. After all, Dad had his own life and his own problems to worry about. Who was I to come in and give him even more issues to deal with? As it turned out, he responded quickly. And positively. Within a week of my request I came home from school to see Mom and Dad sitting together at the dining room table. I joined them.

"So you want to come and live with me, son?" my dad asked.

I nodded yes. Dad continued. "You need to understand something, Josh. I won't make it easy on you. I need you to abide by my rules, no questions asked. And if you fail to follow those rules, there will be consequences." Dad eyed me sternly, but I nodded with even greater enthusiasm.

I remember noticing sadness in Mom's eyes. The transition was bittersweet for her. She grieved one of her boys moving out, but she knew it was for the better. I simply was not becoming the young man that she hoped I would be, and perhaps Dad could make the difference.

Only a week passed before Dad pulled up in his van to help me pack my things and move into his apartment. After loading my stuff, I walked down the hallway to take one more look around my room and make sure that I didn't leave anything behind. Jacob was standing in the middle of the room. He shed no tears, but I could tell that he was hurting.

"I'll miss you, bro," he said.

"I'll miss you too, man."

I wasn't moving far away. Dad's house was only a ten-minute drive from Mom's house. But after years of seeing each other every day for nearly fifteen years, we felt like we were being torn apart. We hugged each other with a long brothers-only type hug. Then I turned and left the room.

My oldest brother Brandon was away at work, but I stopped by Matt's room, where he was jamming out to music. When he finally realized I was standing in his doorway, he walked over and gave me a side hug. He looked me in the eye and said, "Love you, bro." I didn't respond audibly; rather, I smirked at him and nodded my agreement.

Mom waited at the front door. We embraced in silence. I remember her kiss on my cheek before letting go of the hug.

"You are always welcome to come back home if you want to, Josh." Again I saw the sadness in her eyes.

I gave her one more hug and turned to walk out the front door. I hopped into the van where Dad waited. After buckling up I looked over at my father.

"You ready, son?"

"I'm ready, Dad."

He backed out of the driveway and put the car into drive, his eyes fixed on the road ahead. The road that led to my new home with Dad and three years under the healing influence of my hero's love and example. He didn't notice me glance over at him and smile with an expression of joy. I wasn't just travelling to Dad's house for the weekend. I was going on a journey with him that would forever change my life.

Finding a Fixer Upper

Just as I trusted Dad to keep me safe on his motorcycle all those years ago, I now counted on him to pick me up out of the pit I was in. I needed him to communicate my identity. I wanted him to show me my purpose. I was a boy who needed to be fixed, and I believed that my father had all the necessary tools to restore my broken life.

Consider this statement: *The man without a toolbox is a man without a cause.* Or to say it another way, *A man who cannot fix things is purposeless and feels useless.* What do you think about this?

I ask this question to make a point about man. From what I have seen, it is within the nature of man to want to fix things, and if we can't fix, we feel worthless. Fix what? You name it. Fill the blank with anything, and a man feels responsible and hazardously capable to make sure it gets fixed. Fix the car. Fix the garbage disposal. Fix the window. Fix the electric fence. Fix the kid. Fix the... Men want to fix things, and many men try to fix all things. But in truth, there are many things that men can't fix. History testifies that man has never been able to fix the issues of war, racism or poverty. Those problems have haunted man throughout his time here on earth, and they are still tenaciously present today.

Men want to help fix broken women. Husbands hope to fix their broken wives. But in many cases we find that men only cause more damage when trying to fix their women. Here is a truth you can hold onto: *Man cannot fix something that is beyond his capability.* And the truth of the matter is that man, by himself, has no power at all. Consider the words of the Psalmist, "Once God has spoken; twice have I heard this: that power belongs to God" (Psalm 62:11). The point: Man can't fix anything if God does not give him the ability to fix it.

Shortly after I moved in with him, Dad sat me down and asked me what I hoped to receive from him while living under his roof. I told him that I wanted him to fix me. I wanted him to show me my identity. I needed him to tell me my purpose in life. I asked for his direction, precise direction, so that I might know who I am and what I am supposed to do. I thought that if anyone could erase my insecurities and give me a purpose, it would be him.

My request may sound illogical and unfair, but keep in mind that I was asking my hero—a man whom I believed could do anything. I remember arguing with other kids on the playground about whose dad was the strongest. Whose dad was the biggest and best at…whatever. I remember once telling them that my dad could kick a man's head off with his karate skills. (That pretty much ended the debate.) Just like many other children, I adopted the notion that Dad was practically limitless in his ability to accomplish anything he wanted. So it was only natural to assume that he could show me my purpose in life.

Dad, in his wisdom, however, gave me an answer that I did not expect. We were sitting across from each other one afternoon at the dining room table, and he told me, "Son, I don't have the ability to give you what you are asking for. I can't define your purpose and direction. Matter of fact, I can't even tell you what you are truly worth. If you want to have those questions answered, you will have to go to the same person I went to. Only God can tell you what your purpose is. Only God can tell you what you are truly worth."

He illustrated his point by telling me stories about his own life. He told me about the many years when he tried to define his own purpose—one failure upon another. He explained to me why no man can *fully* define another man's purpose. It is true that people can *help* you find your purpose. For instance, a friend can at times help you understand who you are by giving an outside perspective on your personality and character. Such knowledge from a friend can be helpful in providing clues about your purpose in life. But a friend can't assign or fully discern your purpose. *Only God does that, and it is the individual who is solely responsible for seeking God's assignment.* Those were the key points that Dad hoped to communicate to me.

After nearly three hours of talking about purpose I left the conversation with this conclusion: *Every man can live with a self-defined purpose, but if he wants to discover and live for his greatest purpose, he must find that in God.*

Chasing the father Who Chases the Father

Listen to me now, fathers: I am about to share with you something that my father did for me—something that you *must* do for your children. My Dad *showed* me how to chase after my identity and purpose in God by *example*. Before my very eyes, he demonstrated the actions of a man who strives after God. I don't know if he saw me watching him, but what I witnessed in his speech and behavior provided the most significant guidance for my personal, spiritual quest. I watched him wake up in the morning and take time to read God's Word. I passed by his open bedroom door and many times saw him kneeling by his bedside in prayer. I was by his side as he travelled faithfully to church every Sunday morning to give his heart in worship to God. He was a man who did not simply *take* me to church; he was a man who *led* me to church. And I could tell you many other things about the example my father set. Please pay close attention to my point: My dad, *through the way he lived his life*, directed me toward the one true God who could give me identity and purpose.

What are your children witnessing in your example? Where are you leading them? You may say here that you do not have any children to be an example for. But God presents us opportunities every day. Young boys who were just like me cross your path all the time. I believe that some of these young men have been intentionally placed near you by God. He hopes that you will invest your life in the boy who knows everything about fatherlessness and nothing about a heavenly Father. I understand that many of us feel unworthy and ill-equipped to lead young men to God. But a boy in search of purpose and identity does not need a man that has all the answers. He only needs a man that is willing to point toward the God who holds the answers.

Here is a truth about my father: He is a very plain and simple man. He does not hold a prestigious job. He does not have a hefty bank account. He has, like many men, lived a past full of failure and regret. In the sense of worldly accomplishment, my father has achieved little. But I am certain that when I join him in the eternal kingdom of heaven, I will find that he has acquired everlasting blessing and possession far above anything this world could ever hope to offer.

This blessing that my father has acquired is the same that I hope to acquire myself. As Dad's son, I learned to read the Bible just like he did. And in reading that Bible I found that there is a life filled with insurmountable blessing for those who chase after God. In my opinion, Dad did everything he could to point me towards God in the short time that I lived with him. For three years I was in the presence of a man who sought God fervently. Shortly before I moved out, I remember Dad talking with me about my own personal choices and direction in life. He said to me, "Son, whatever you choose to do or wherever you choose to go with your life, just know this: No matter what, I believe in you and I love you. Ultimately, there is just one thing that I selfishly hope for with you."

"What's that, Dad?" I asked him.

"Just meet me on the other side, son."

I thought about his words and their significance. Though Dad would continue to influence my life, we were now at an important parting of the ways. I was preparing to leave his home and walk the journey of life without his constant presence. I would begin to establish my own standards and practices in direct dependence on my heavenly Father. Dad and Mom would no longer be there to lead me by the hand. It was time to start making my own choices, leaning, of course, even more heavily on the Lord. Time to start living my life as I saw fit—guided by my own understanding of God's direction. Time to find my identity and purpose by chasing after God for myself.

I was once a son who chased after my earthly father. It was God who made it possible for me to catch him, and I am eternally grateful. So much would have been missing within me had I not experienced those few short years living with Dad. He didn't, by his own hand, give me the identity and purpose that I hoped for. But He pointed me toward the cross of Christ. A cross where God sacrificed Himself so that we might have purpose and meaning. With this sacrifice in mind, it was time for me to stop chasing my earthly father so that I could wholly focus on chasing my heavenly Father.

Part II

A SON AND HIS FATHER

Chapter 8

CHOICES, CHOICES

—⁓—

We're bombarded with so many decisions, each day carries new risk of getting it wrong. We mortal creatures are only able to see so far ahead when trying to determine how our choices will impact the future. Oddly enough, sometimes the seemingly best decisions can lead to the worst consequences and vice versa. Anyone who has lived for some years on this crazy planet knows that life can be a chancy thing. And this brings us to one of the great beauties of life: Risks aren't all bad. Through taking risks *in obedience to God*, we get to live life in abundance and perhaps find the purpose of our lives, even in the foggiest of circumstances.

Thanks to my father, finding a purpose in my life was not as challenging as it could have been. Because of the foundation Dad provided by his example, I embarked on a different path from the one I would have chosen if Dad hadn't stepped in as my hero. I had learned from my dad to put God first and foremost in my life. I had learned to be like Dad, who was learning to be like Jesus, in the most important ways. The rest of this book is about the ways that Dad's influence, as a son chasing after his Father, has guided many aspects of my life as a son of God.

Without question, children are greatly blessed when they have fathers who learned to prioritize life rightly. Children gain wisdom from the father who has figured out God's road is the best road to walk. It may not be the easy road, but as we search for the road that God would have us travel upon we are in search for the best possible road. But God's road is never free of struggles.

It's not unusual for trouble to arise just when you discover God's will for your life. Kind of a good-news-bad-news situation. The good news: You found what God wants. The bad news: You may not want what God wants. But with God the good news always trumps the bad news, for God brings an eternal plan that leads heavenward, not a temporary plan that leads to the grave.

As you seek to discover God's plan you may disagree with His direction for your life. His plan may not match up with your own wishes and dreams. But in all honesty, our own dreams are commonly selfish dreams that we have conjured up in our minds for ourselves. Our selfishness can get in the way of finding God's way for our lives. And there is also the issue of other people. The input of well-intentioned people could lead us away from what God wants because they too may not like His plan for our lives. Allow me to explain what I mean.

God's Way Is the High Way

I met my best friend, Joanne, when I was seventeen years old. Like a fool, I had absolutely no romantic interest in her at the time. I wasn't interested in any girls; I was hoping to get my head on straight before considering the opposite sex romantically.

I communicated this relationship status with her in a sort of backhanded way—I lost her phone number three separate times. Lord, oh Lord, did I almost miss out on something big.

Time passed and our friendship blossomed. We would talk on the phone for hours. Just having her on the other end of the line made me content with life. I remember one conversation in particular with Joanne. We were wrapping up and I, being one of those guys who sometimes speaks before he thinks, just laid it out on the phone:

"I love you, Joanne."

Click.

"Hello?"

Thus went my first confession of love to her. She called back shortly after, asking me what I said. "Nothing," I answered. We still laugh about that conversation.

Ever so slowly I discovered that Joanne was the woman for me. I was in love with the Lord, and falling in love with her. She had become the one I intended to marry. But several circumstances seemed to bode poorly for that course of action. I was only twenty years old with minimal education under my belt. I held a job with little security and was living with my grandparents. By the world's standard, I was clearly unready for marriage and the commitment that went with it. But I sought God's will in prayer, and I felt Him telling me that Joanne was the woman for me, and that marriage was nearer than I thought. I sensed that I was supposed to trust God and believe that He would work out the details. That was my understanding at least.

Maybe you can guess how my family responded to my convinced mind.

For months I met only friction. I was bombarded with statistics about the current divorce rates, the cost of rent and daily survival, how important a college education was before getting married and starting a family, and so forth. I couldn't disagree with any of those arguments. They were all valid points. But I had learned from my father not to do things by the world's standard, but by God's standard. If you are one who reads Scripture, I am sure you have picked up on the fact that *God does not usually call the capable or even the ready; rather, he calls the one who simply loves Him, and is willing to stick his neck out in faith for his God.* That was the kind of calling I was sensing. Perhaps you have sensed the same kind of calling from Him as well. It can be hard to "just trust God" when many around you are telling you that you are going to ruin your life. Don't get me wrong, I think that the counsel of loved ones is important to consider since "many advisers bring success" (Proverbs 15:22, NLT), but sometimes their counsel comes from their own perspective rather than from God's.

So there I was with a strong sense of surety, believing that I was supposed to marry Joanne. But in spite of my confidence, Joanne and I nearly called off the wedding since my father was unwilling to give his blessing. Mom had already given her blessing, but Dad would not budge on his conviction that I was making a big mistake. I couldn't blame him; I also saw the "logic" in not getting married, given my apparent circumstances. All I had was a strong feeling of being called to marry Joanne, a dangerous thing to trust by itself. We can sometimes trick ourselves into thinking that we hear God when, in fact, we are hearing anything but Him. What is more, God commands in Scripture that we honor our parents. And marrying Joanne violated that command if I didn't have both parents' blessings. I needed clear evidence from God showing me that I should marry Joanne, since I had so many things going against me. After all, Next to choosing God, choosing a wife is the biggest decision one can make in life.

And so I set a deadline and said to God, *Unless I get Dad's blessing by this date, I'm calling the wedding off.* I was serious.

Two months passed, and the deadline came. It was a Sunday, and things were not looking "sunny" for Joanne and me.

But that's when God revealed what He'd known all along: It was just a matter of timing. On the very day that I needed Dad's blessing, a gentleman at church named Tim went and talked with my father. He had no knowledge of the deadline I had set with God, nor was he aware of my condition for receiving Dad's blessing before marrying Joanne. He said to me later that he was simply moved by the Holy Spirit to speak with Dad about how important it had been to him—to Tim, that is—to get his own dad's blessing on his marriage. Tim's dad never had given his blessing, but in the end, Tim married his bride anyway, and they are still happily married to this day. Unfortunately, His relationship with his father was no longer so happy. That Sunday, after hearing Tim's story, Dad conceded and gave his blessing.

You can call it coincidence if you like, but I believe God intervened that day.

God has a purpose and a plan for each of our lives. His plan might make little sense to us and even lesser sense to others. But when we are looking for His way, God will, somehow or other, help us see whether we are going His direction. I am not saying that God's will always works out from the world's perspective. Things can get ugly sometimes as we strive to go God's way, as was the case for Tim and his dad. That is one of the risks you take when chasing after God. When we go after God, we may sacrifice our reputation with the world—even with people close to us—but we will likely gain an honorable life. As a matter of fact, we do gain an honorable life, not necessarily in the world's eyes, but in the eyes that really count, God's eyes.

If you choose to become a son or daughter who chases the Father, you may be challenged to take a risk from time to time, or to give something up. But taking the obedient risk and making the Spirit-prompted sacrifice opens doors to eternal treasures even greater than any earthly treasure you might lose. God never promises that all of our decisions will be easy. But *persistent obedience, especially through the toughest terrain of life, will prompt God to open His floodgates and abundantly pour out something invaluably greater than anything the world could ever offer—spiritual blessing—over our lives.*

Go Where?!

We all know that we have inadequacies and weaknesses. When we humbly recognize our inadequacies, we should be inspired to mature those infuriating character weaknesses. We all have skills and traits that require strengthening and growth, and sometimes God takes us on an intense path to make us the men (or women) we are supposed to be. Such was the case for me.

At age thirteen, I got involved in sales. I sold subscriptions for the *Columbian* newspaper. I was the kid who would come knocking at your door and plead with you to buy my valuable product so that I could "go to Disneyland" or "save up for my college education." I had a real knack for pushing a product, so as a young adult I consciously chose sales as my career path. For ten years I remained in the sales gig, going from job to job, wherever the money was. I was content and by no means looking for a new direction in my life. I knew, however, that God held a direction for my life.

Wouldn't it be nice if we could go to the local vendor and buy a map which navigates our way to God's will? But the possibility of such a purchase does not exist. Only God holds that roadmap, and we are called to place our life in His Hands and follow His directions. I was quite sure that I was willing to go God's way. But my confident assumption was about to be challenged, no holds barred. God was about to ask me, *Are you really ready for My next step for you?*

Throughout the six years since we'd met, Joanne and I had attended church together. (Church is a good place to find a godly spouse.) Our needs were met, and we were doing pretty well in our marriage. It didn't seem to me like a time for change.

One Sunday morning, after six years of Sunday morning church services, God put a sudden calling on Joanne's heart. In the middle of service, Joanne felt the Holy Spirit telling her, *You are supposed to join the military.* It had nothing to do with the pastor's message or any other aspect of the service. It was just an impression that she suddenly got.

On the car ride home from church, Joanne spoke up. "I think we are supposed to join the military."

I swallowed hard and looked at her. You see, I also had felt this impression during the church service. The calling had come from out of nowhere. I couldn't believe I'd heard her correctly. I never thought I'd consider the military, and I had planned to keep my mouth shut about the whole *weird impression* thing. The Army recruiters used to call me at home and tell me what a great career they could offer. My response to them always ended the same way—with the *click* of a hang-up. I simply wasn't interested.

In my prideful thinking, I had enough skills to survive and even thrive in this simple world. I had no need for Uncle Sam to get behind me and help support my and my family's needs. What a poor attitude I had, blinded by arrogance. However, that Sunday morning started me rethinking my attitude. I asked God, *Is this something You are calling me to, Lord?* I wasn't yet sold on the idea of joining the service. Sure I felt a little tug on my heart, and Joanne did as well, but couldn't that just be coincidence?

As I said before, in life's big decisions we need more than a feeling. I believe all of us can at times sense the Holy Spirit, and make wise decisions when we submit to the Holy Spirit's leading. But there are just some decisions that require more. If this was God, he was asking me to sign my life away. That was not part of my plan, not a part of the life I wanted.

Nevertheless I prayed, *If this is Your calling, Lord, then I need clear direction. I need more than a feeling. I need You to show me that this is what you want.*

I was asking God for some sort of manifestation, maybe a miracle that would help my faith in making a decision this big. Much like Gideon, I suppose, who asked God to make the fleece wet and the ground dry. And after God did that, Gideon asked Him, if the Lord would be so kind, to do the opposite, as yet another proof (Judges 6:36-40). We can ask God for some ridiculous evidence, but I don't think He minds, if our hearts are right.

A week passed, and another Sunday morning came. Joanne and I scheduled a meeting with our pastor after service. We spoke with him about God's apparent leading, what we were feeling and sensing. He gave us sound advice: to continue to pray and seek counsel from other people. Our pastor did not say anything definitive like, "Yes, God is telling you to join the military." Or, "Don't believe it, you two, not for a second. It is a lie from Satan himself." He just said, "Continue to seek God, and trust Him." It was good advice, but as Joanne and I left, we were still unsure what to do. I was already beginning to have doubts about the *feeling* I had gotten only a week ago. I was starting to think, *Maybe it was just a coincidence.* Time can do that when you don't want to go somewhere or do something. You start to look for ways out. *Even if the voice of God resonates clearly, what our rebel ears choose to hear may change as we delay.*

After meeting with the pastor, Joanne and I decided to hit up one of our favorite Chinese restaurants. There I noticed something peculiar—four marines looking all spiffy in their blue dress uniforms, eating in the back corner of the restaurant. It was an odd sight; one seldom sees military in uniform in Gresham, Oregon. Even odder was the fact that they were out on a Sunday afternoon, a day when most military are off duty. I didn't think too much of seeing them at first. Joanne and I sat down and started looking over the menus. I tried to decide on something to eat, but I couldn't stop wondering why those four marines were there. The more I thought about it, the stranger it seemed.

Then I heard the voice: *Why don't you go ask them why they are here?*

I knew who was asking me. I thought about it, and I decided to endure the social awkwardness and be obedient. I got up from my seat and walked over to the marines. They stopped eating and looked up at me. They probably thought I was there to thank them for their service. (We should always remember to do that.) Instead I said, "I know this may sound like a weird question, but why are you guys here?"

One of the gentlemen smiled with a big grin. "You know, that's a good question," he said. "We just woke up this morning and felt like going out to lunch together." I stood listening, little knowing that God was about to use this man to hit me between the eyes. "We drove around for a while looking for a place to eat and felt *compelled* to come here. And so, here we are."

My mind started lighting up like a Christmas tree. I had asked for revelation, and revelation I got. I thanked the gentleman and walked away, convinced now about where I was called to go next.

Some will call this a coincidence. Sure, military go out to eat on Sunday afternoons, and sometimes they dress up in uniform. I've done it. But this involved too many "coincidences" to be mere coincidence. An event like this occurs within one week of asking God to prove His will to me. The marine used the word "compelled," and they chose to wake up one random morning and go out to eat...in uniform...while off duty...at the same restaurant that Joanne and I happened to choose. On top of all that, it was two PM, a time when few people are out to lunch. And then calculate the chances that both Joanne and I would "sense" the same leading, apparently from God, on the same day. Chances are slim, my friend, very slim. And if you are one who does not believe that God reveals things to us plainly at times, perhaps you should stop reading this book, as I am preparing to talk in the next chapter about some things that will sound just plain crazy to you.

The point I am trying to get at here is simple: *God has a will for my life, for your life, for every life.* God means to take us on a journey that will produce unforeseen growth. We were created for a specific purpose but whether or not we fulfill that purpose is up to us. The most meaningful life we can have is the one held in the hands of God, and I can tell you that surrendering to God is a chance worth taking, and a choice worth making.

But it is your choice.

Whoever Loses His Life for My Sake...

Joanne and I had made the decision together to join the military. Joanne didn't take the oath of enlistment, but as my wife she was just as much in the military as I was. We had to prepare our hearts and minds for the challenging journey that laid ahead. It was a stressful time, and as the day neared for me to take the oath of enlistment, I noticed a further rise in tensions. Though Joanne and I were fully convinced, with no plans of turning back, most of my family was fully committed to changing our minds. The only person who fully supported Joanne and me was my Dad. I still remember his words to me when I told him I was joining the service: "Son, I trust that you can make the right decision for yourself. You are your own man now. I believe that you have the wisdom to know when God is speaking to you and have total confidence that you will succeed in anything you do." Those words stick with me still now. I hope you can communicate the same kind of words to your own children.

It was 2004, three years after 9/11. The US was still in a hot war. Troops were dying on a daily basis, literally giving their all for their country. My oldest brother, Brandon, was the most passionate about keeping us from joining. Any time Big Brother came around, he was sure to tell stories of chaplains who almost got blown up, trainees who were thrown into the ocean and told to swim back or die (and the trainers meant it), and horrible hazings of new recruits. He made a hobby of trying to scare us out of joining the military.

Mom hated the idea, too. She would plead with me saying, "Please don't join, Josh; the chance is too great that you might die."

This tension went on for months, with only my dad's support on my side of the family. Joanne's family, having a military background, supported our decision fully. From my mom and brothers, though, the most I got was my little brother reservedly saying, "I guess, just do whatever God tells you." Almost my entire family is Christian, yet here they were telling me that, regardless of my conviction, I was crazy to join.

We set up a time for all of us—except Dad, who had to work—to sit down together and discuss our differences. I never told my family about the four marines at the restaurant or what God had showed to me to clarify His will. I wanted my family to support me on their own, without a story. I wanted them in my corner, even if they didn't like the corner. Looking back on it now I can see that I was being selfish. But I needed to know that my family trusted and respected my decisions without having to hear a miraculous story.

There we all were, together again. It had been quite a while since the four brothers and Mom had all sat down together in the living room of our home. The home where we grew up together, made memories, bonded together and loved each other. This gathering, however, while memorable, wouldn't be a warm memory; my mom and brothers intended to convince me of my audacity at leaving the family, my home and one another's close proximity. Around the circle, each person expressed his or her opinion as to why Joanne and I shouldn't leave. I listened carefully to their hearts, while the whole process was breaking my own. They each gave their reasoning—good reasoning—and then came my turn.

I started telling them why I personally wanted to join the military. I'd only gotten five sentences out before Brandon interrupted me. "It's just that we don't want you to die."

I remember the look in his eyes as he said it. There was anguish on his face and deep concern in his eyes. It was clear that he believed his little brother was in grave danger. Tears welled up in my eyes when I recognized his fear for me. The depth of my brother's words leveled my heart. The love of a family can go deep, very deep, and my brother was reaching into my chest and squeezing my heart in that moment. It was painful—really painful. But loving.

I could hardly push out the words after seeing my biggest brother's concern, but the words had to be said. Something even bigger than the family's love and cohesion was happening here. God was calling Joanne and me out to be obedient to His will, regardless of the difficulty and the danger. Maybe that is part of what Jesus meant when He said, "Do not think that I have come to bring peace to the earth. I have not come to bring peace, but a sword. For I have come to set a man against his father, and a daughter against her mother, and a daughter-in-law against her mother-in-law. And a person's enemies will be those of his own household. Whoever loves father or mother more than me is not worthy of me, and whoever loves son or daughter more than me is not worthy of me" (Matthew 10:34-37).

These are some seriously strong words by the Christ. My parents and brothers weren't my enemies, but Jesus' meaning still applied: We are to love and choose His will for our lives above all else. *Absolutely nothing should come before His will for us, to include our families' feelings.* For this reason, I had to tell my family that I was going to do what God was leading me to do, and that Joanne and I were making that decision together. It was one of the hardest conversations I've had to endure in my life.

Though the tensions were high then, time helped my family become more accepting of my decision. I don't think they fully accepted it until the day I actually left for basic training. That's when they realized that my word was my bond. I missed home while I was at training; I missed it throughout the four years of active duty. But I was doing what God had called me to do, and I found deep contentment in that.

That is what you will find when you do what God calls you to do—contentment. I can say now that because of God helping me along in the decision to join the Air Force, I have been made a better and stronger man in the areas where I was weak. When you go God's way, He makes you stronger, makes you better than the man you were yesterday. God's will for our lives does not always line up with the opinions or desires of our family or closest friends. God's calling may cause you to lose friends or make enemies—maybe both at the same time. He could call you into a place where you will be despised and rejected by loved ones. He may even call you into a place that *looks* like nothing but darkness and despair to you. *But it is in that place that God and His glorious light may very well reside.*

We may not see God's light and the purpose of His ways until we are willing to step into danger, step into the darkness, or step into the fire, as God required of Shadrach, Meshach and Abednego in Daniel 3. These were men of faith, unwilling to bow down to any god but the one True God. It is interesting that the Lord did not choose to prevent these men of faith from entering the fiery furnace. Rather, He met them *inside* the furnace (Daniel 3:24-25). *Perhaps God wants to meet you in the same kind of place.* He calls out to those listening to take a chance and trust on Him. He says, "Whoever would save his life will lose it, but whoever loses his life for my sake will find it" (Matthew 16:25). So we can say, even when facing possible death, we are nonetheless called to follow God in faith and courage. And though many have said that it is getting harder to see God these days, if we chase after Him—if we strive to move each day closer to Him—we will sooner or later find Him in clear view.

And He'll be smiling.

Chapter 9

BUT IS GOD REAL?

I promised in the last chapter to mention some things that many would find crazy. I too would think them crazy had they not happened to me. Sometimes that's the realm in which God operates, the realm of crazy. I know that I am asking a lot of you in this book (and not just I necessarily, but God as well). I am asking that you place your trust in God, not just in part, but in full. Since I make such a lofty request, you should know something more about me.

In all honesty, I wrestle daily with choosing to do God's will. I have also wrestled *heavily* with the question of God's existence in such a broken world. I too have lacked the faith to do the tasks that God calls me to do. Sometimes I screw up altogether, doing the exact opposite of what God has asked of me.

In short, I too am a man. And together, as men (and women) we are a race that doubts God, and not completely without good reason. That is why I write this chapter to you, to offer evidence for God's existence. I do not plan to use creationist arguments or scientific and philosophical proofs. I just want to tell you a few stories from my experience.

After God first revealed himself to me (in the shower of all places; see Chapter 2), He for some reason continued periodically to do it (not usually in the shower). I have seen some unusual sights in my life—sights that, experienced first-hand, would strengthen anyone's faith in God and the spirit world. I have seen both sides, the light and the dark, and I am not sure which to describe first. I suppose I should finish with the side of greater power, so first I will relate two times when I have come into close proximity with the darkness.

The Side of Darkness

Dad was not the only parent who helped teach me the all-important lesson of chasing after God. Mom also shared hugely in helping me see what matters most. She was busy at work much of the time, and then she also had the responsibilities of keeping up the house and caring for four boys. I remember her constantly cleaning the house, cooking meals from scratch, coming out to soccer games, and (I cringe in guilt) doing multiple chores that her boys failed to accomplish. This list could go on, but what I didn't know until my late teens was that she was deeply committed to prayer. Every night while she lay in bed by herself, she would send up silent prayers to God for her boys. Each of my brothers and I skirted dangerously near the edge of destruction. Any one of us could easily have turned to drugs, parties, alcohol or any of the world's other deadly temptations. I have come to believe that her prayers helped rescue us from a life of misery and foolishness.

It was not easy for her, day after day filling the role of both parents. Family is never supposed to operate that way, but it did for her. I think sometimes that Mom lost her sanity so that we brothers could keep ours. It had to be taxing on her soul at times. I think that was one of the reasons she recommitted herself to the Lord through baptism. She decided to say once again to her God that she was sold out for Him. And she continually, faithfully recommitted herself to Him as a conscious decision every day. Even to this day, she is a woman of exemplary faith.

As I mentioned, Mom did a good job keeping the house clean, even with four young boys terrorizing the home without mercy. As in any home, the occasional fly or two would join us during summer; we usually kept the windows open to cool the house. This sets the scene for the strange, unforgettable event that occurred the same night Mom rededicated her life to God.

We arrived home and Mom unlocked and opened the front door to a swarm of flies like I had never seen before, and hope never to see again. I'm talking swarms upon swarms of huge, nasty flies. I'm guessing there were more than a thousand in all. I wasn't counting; it may have been many thousands. They covered the dining room table, the windows, the kitchen counters. The flies were literally everywhere. The only thing that stands out stronger in my memory from that night than the flies is the look on my mother's face—a look of horror. To me, at the time at least, the flies weren't a big deal. My two older brothers actually went running into the house, looking for ways to eradicate the flies from our home. Their methods were somewhat grotesque. They turned out all the lights and opened the microwave. The flies were attracted to the microwave's light, and once fifteen or twenty had flown in, my brothers would close the microwave and nuke 'em. I'm glad that I didn't have to clean that thing out…

Looking back on that night, I'm now convinced that the swarm of flies was a demonic manifestation. One of Satan's names in the Bible is Beelzebub or Beelzebul, which can be translated "lord of the flies" (see for example Luke 11:15, 18-19). Sure, there are possible natural explanations: Maybe something in the house attracted the flies, or maybe they had been nesting unseen in something that went bad, and just happened to emerge all at once that night. But of all the possible times, it seems odd that they would show up on the night that Mom rededicated her life to God. And Mom's face displayed more than disgust; she was deeply frightened.

That was the first time I saw a sight that I can't easily explain, an event that might very well have been supernatural, from the originator of evil. A second story raises the inexplicability bar several notches further.

When I was seventeen, I committed to attending youth group. Week after week I would go and hear the message and participate in the fun. After youth group I would always come home, sit down on the couch and have a snack while watching some TV. This went on for months without incident, until one summer night. I arrived home from youth group, opened the door and stepped into my apartment. I felt a sudden tension upon entering. It was the first time I ever came home and suddenly felt something *off*. What I felt is hard to explain. It was as though a cloud of darkness was shrouding my apartment and had settled in to stay. I felt like I was stepping into that cloud. The apartment lights were on, but the room still felt dark. (I don't know how better to explain it.)

Even stranger than the feeling of darkness was the... something... that I first glimpsed out of the left corner of my eye. It was moving across the room, a shadow of sorts crawling along the dining room wall behind the table. Assuming my mind was playing tricks on me, I looked across the room at the shadow. I watched intensely as it moved another foot along the wall and then stopped. I couldn't believe what I was seeing; I stood and stared. It had a body with arms and legs, but no hands or feet. The arms I remember most clearly, as they were bent in a contorted way. The upper arms went straight out from the shoulders while the lower arms pointed straight down. And the thing had no head. It freaked me out big time. I remember the hairs on my arms standing up and my fists clenching. Even though this entity had no eyes, I could feel it staring back at me, as though challenging me: *Now you see me. What are you going to do about it?*

I opened up my mouth and said, "In the name of Jesus Christ, get out of this house. You do not belong here."

I stood my ground as I said the words and continued to stare the shadow down. After a few seconds' pause, the shadow began to move jaggedly along the wall again. It was creepy. Nevertheless, the demonic manifestation made its way out; it seeped through the nearby open window and disappeared into the night. The room's atmosphere changed. Somehow I knew in my heart that that thing would not be back, but I was changed forever in that moment.

I don't think anyone can say anything to convince me that a spiritual realm does not exist. I don't mean to be closed-minded about the issue. I think that sound logic is critical, and a gift from God. But when I came into contact with that spiritual force, I was presented with new, unquestionable data, and logic now threw any doubts I'd harbored about the spiritual reality out the window (pun intended).

So there I was, with a newly confirmed conviction that real spiritual evil exists. I believe that it lives among us, usually unseen. (Sorry if that creeps you out.) I don't know *all* the purposes and activities of these evil spirits. I've taken Angelology and Demonology in Bible College to get some good ideas about what they do and where they come from. We know that they are fallen angels who once willfully chose to reject God, and they are now continually at war with the soldiers of God's kingdom—the angels who've remained faithful to God.

And speaking of God's angels…

The Side of Light

As a young boy, one of my favorite TV shows was *Unsolved Mysteries*. Sometimes I would foolishly watch it alone with the lights out and get the crud scared out of me. I remember thinking, *I bet one of those killers is right outside lurking in my back yard. I* believed at times that the murderer was going to come through my screen door. I thought, *I'm finished for sure.* We can conjure up some strange thoughts as children (and as paranoid adults). Anyway, my favorite portion of the show was about unexplained mysteries regarding spiritual matters. The show documented stories of people who were convinced they were a reincarnation of someone from the past. Some of their stories sounded pretty convincing. There were also stories of people moving into homes and having their plates thrown around by invisible beings. Stories of people coming back from the afterlife, having met God or encountered the proverbial bright light.

I also remember several segments about angels. One guy told a story of how his car fell off the jack while he was under it, and some random 'stranger' lifted the car off him. He suffered cracked ribs, but if the stranger hadn't been there, the guy would surely have died. His rescuer suddenly vanished, and he was convinced that an angel had helped him.

I didn't know what to think of the many angel stories I heard throughout my childhood. I grew up in church, where I was taught about the possibility of angels and the messages that they sometimes brought. For example, the angel Gabriel brought the message of hope to the world, telling Mary that the Christ was to be born through her (Luke 1:26-38). But when you really get down to it and think about things angels do or have done, these stories honestly seem like something out of a fairy tale. Short of first-hand experience, who could blame someone for believing that angels are simply the products of creative human minds? I used to think that was the possible explanation for angels. I think we all doubt to some degree whether or not a metaphysical world operates outside the world we see. Why else are we surprised when the supernatural shows up? For me, an episode in my late teens would catch me completely unaware and confirm the existence of these angelic beings.

While living with Dad, I started going to church with him every Sunday. The worship was pretty intense, and the messages were great. It was the first church I ever attended that expressed real feeling and depth of heart in their worship. I'm sure some of the other churches had the same kind of heart; they just didn't expressively show it as much.

I went to this church many Sundays; I was on fire and in love with the Lord. The demonic manifestation I'd seen in my apartment helped me realize that God's love was protecting me from some serious evil. (It is a love that protects you from evil as well.) I loved to worship God; I still love worshiping Him. I was wholly convinced that He existed, and even more than that, that He was with me, in my heart. I was in a good place.

I have plenty of friends who say, "You know, I'm open to believing in God. If only He would show Himself to me in such and such a way, then I would definitely believe in Him." I don't understand fully why God does not reveal Himself plainly to everyone. Maybe it is because He doesn't care so much that we are convinced of His basic existence; even demons and unbelievers can know that He exists (James 2:19). Perhaps He's more concerned about whether or not we're genuinely placing our *faith* in Him. Whatever the case maybe, I was about to learn one Sunday—a day when my faith was both rewarded and bolstered—God provides plenty of evidence for those who are willing to look around.

On that Sunday, as the church service was coming to an end, I could no longer ignore the call of nature—a call of some urgency. So I left the service a little early. As I went down the stairs toward the bathroom, I saw a tall and broad gentleman standing outside the glass main doors of the building. My need to use the restroom dissipated as my curiosity piqued at seeing the man standing alone. The guy wore plain jeans and a button-down shirt. He stood a good six feet, plus another five to seven inches to boot. He must have weighed around 240 pounds. He was not fat by any means, but he was large and had a look of significant strength. Could have been an effective bouncer, I suppose. He sported red hair, a red mustache (an impressive one) and pale skin. Since I considered myself one of the church's greeters, I thought it good to introduce myself to him. As I opened the door, I recall a powerful presence suddenly coming upon me. It felt like I was stepping into a court of majesty. I remember feeling my skin tingle as I stepped outside. The door closed behind me, and I felt like I was inside a bubble with this man; no one else was invited to enter. I didn't say a word as I stood next to him. He didn't speak either. He just kept looking into the sky. I knew that he knew I was there, but he just kept staring upward, so I did the same. For what seemed five minutes we held our pose.

After some time passed he finally turned his head and looked at me to say, "It's beautiful, isn't it?"

"Yes, it is." That's all I could say.

I knew he was making a statement about God's creation. Just that stunning and beautiful clear sky that stood before us pronounced God's existence. Looking upward into the sky causes me to feel at times that I'm looking in the direction that I am meant to, that I'm created to. We gazed admiringly a while longer before I turned and looked through the glass door into the church. The service was over, and there was a crowd of people already out in fellowship. I remember thinking, *how did everyone get downstairs so quickly without me noticing and why didn't they come out side to meet with me and the guy I was standing by.* I spotted my dad as I looked through the glass where everyone was congregating.

"Hey," I said, "I want you to meet someone." I pointed toward the emerging crowd.

The guy looked at me but didn't say anything. I took it as a cue to invite my dad. I opened the door and called out, "Hey, Dad, come here. I want you to meet someone."

Dad was at the cross way of the door within seconds but he looked at me and my surroundings curiously. He asked, "Meet who, son?"

I'd had my back turned for, maybe, seven seconds. When I turned again to look for my accompanying sky gazer, he was gone. I mean *gone.* At first I thought someone was playing a trick on me. I ran around the corner of the building, just a few feet away, the only place this guy could possibly have hidden. He wasn't there. The only other terrain in all directions was open fields.

I was stupefied, to say the least. My dad was still looking at me, wondering what was going on. I didn't know what to say. I told Dad about what had just transpired and he said, "That's pretty amazing." Amazing indeed!

And yes, I did eventually make it to the restroom.

I still wonder sometimes why God did that for me—allowed me to see one of His ministering spirits first-hand. I wonder if perhaps the angel I met is my guardian, since Scripture does allude to such beings and their personal assignments (Psalm 91:11; Matthew 18:10). Guardian angels would help explain the many crazy dangers my brothers and I have survived without consequence. I can hardly count the number of times that we should have been seriously injured, or even missed our next birthday.

I know that these stories of demons and angels can sound absurd and unbelievable. There was a time when such tales would have sounded like fables to me too. But my skepticism has been silenced since I've experienced the supernatural firsthand.

Whether or not you want to believe these stories is up to you. Frankly, you believing my report is not critically important to me. What is critically important is your decision to believe in God and place genuine faith in Him. *These stories are meant to point you toward the possibility of God, or even to bring you into a deeper conviction that God does indeed exist.* I'm like the truthful witness in the courtroom, absolutely convinced of what I've seen and its conclusions, sharing it with you, the jury. Even if no one else comes to believe in the supernatural because of these stories, I know without any doubt that it does exist. I share nonetheless, in hopes that my testimony might strengthen your faith as well.

Yes, my friend, I am fully confident that God is alive, and I believe that somehow you know it too. I believe that something in you tells you that this world simply couldn't be possible unless there was a mastermind behind it all. Certainly death, despair, tragedy, famine, pestilence, murder, adultery, abortion and all other horrors of humanity—they all exist. But they don't necessarily deny God's existence. Rather, they prove our humanity and demonstrate still further our need of a higher power to protect us from ourselves. We live in a tragic place. This world's trials can be a relentless weight bearing down on us. And even though we all feel the weight, I am quite sure that God is only allowing as much pressure to come down on each of us as He wills or allows. After all, it is through high temperature and tremendous pressure that diamonds are naturally formed.

Chapter 10

TRYING TO MAKE SENSE
OF TRAGEDY

Even if we acknowledge God's existence, the trials that He allows in our lives sometimes seem beyond a human's ability to bear. If you've walked "through the valley of the shadow of death," as King David termed it (Psalm 23:4), or if you've experienced some other serious loss or trauma, you know exactly what I mean. The sorrow seems unending, overwhelming, beyond human comprehension. We commonly respond with bewilderment, anger, grief and, sometimes, hopelessness. Tragedy's road lies through a dry, lonely desert, where tears fall on dust and disappear instantly into the thirsty ground. Nothing grows there; all of life's terrain seems barren, worthless.

I've seen people's despair often in my line of work. An Air Force chaplain assistant gets to see many of the heavy burdens that the men and women in uniform carry. The years they give in service are among the greatest sacrifices one can make. As they raise their hands in oath to defend democracy and freedom, they are giving up more than themselves. They are giving up Sunday afternoon barbecues with the family. They are giving up the close proximity of Mom and Dad, brother and sister, aunt and uncle—the family that was always close at hand for hugs in all seasons. Home—a place of familiarity and comfort—is suddenly whisked away. It's in this context of displacement and foreignness that tragedy can have its greatest impact upon young men and women in service.

You might think that the most common tragedy for someone in the military would be loss and trauma from the battlefield. And for many, it is. But consider also what it's like for service personnel to experience the unexpected loss of a loved one at such a distance. I remember many airmen coming into the chapel overwhelmed with this kind of tragedy. The unforeseen death of a close family member weighs even heavier on those who are away from home in uniform. Perhaps two or three years have passed since they visited home, and suddenly they receive notice of their loss while standing on some airbase across the country or on the other side of the world. They've never felt so far from home.

Such was the case for my dear friend—we'll call him Daniel—who served honorably in the army. His grandfather endured an extended battle with cancer for eight years. "The day I found out," he told me, "I was at Sam Barlow High School for my brother's baseball game. I was getting ready to eat something from the snack shack when I first heard that Grandpa was sick. I lost my appetite."

The memory of that devastating revelation clung to my friend and seemed completely unwilling to let go. Maybe you can relate? Maybe you've received tragic news that keeps playing over and over in your head. Every time the memory is triggered you feel the tension in your spirit once again. You remember the sights, the smells, the atmosphere around you. You feel as though you're transported back into the past, to that moment of emotional ambush, that moment of utter helplessness.

The news of his grandfather's cancer made this kind of tragic impact on Daniel. He was devastated. You see, as my friend entered his teens, he and his grandpa built a strong relationship. Both of them were interested in God, and they talked about the Bible all the time. First Peter was their favorite book to discuss. Their relationship exemplified the potential for a grandfather and a grandson. In his journey through adolescence, Daniel securely fastened his hand into his grandfather's and trusted his wisdom. Grandpa was there to guide and counsel his grandson through the troubling teenage years. He helped plant his grandson's feet on the Rock, Jesus Christ. He became Daniel's hero, just as my own father became my hero. With the help of his grandfather, Daniel became a man who wanted to honor his God by walking a life worthy of the Lord.

Inspired, Daniel searched out God's calling and ended up joining the army immediately out of high school. He aspired to become a medic and scored well enough to be classed for the job he wanted. He made it through basic training with no issues and started his schooling. Things were going in the right direction for him. Life was looking bright as he walked the path to which God had called him.

But then in the middle of his training Daniel got the news: Grandpa was being put on hospice. He had about three months to live. Upon hearing the news, the grandson yearned to run back home to his dying mentor, but the gap between Texas and Idaho, where his grandfather now resided, was too large. Unless death was a sure thing, Daniel would have to stay and finish his schooling or risk being reclassed into a new job. He knew what his grandpa would want him to do. My friend continued his training.

With the weighty knowledge of his grandfather's condition and the passing of a little time, Daniel began struggling with sin. A young single guy in the army usually faces peer pressure to do the wrong things. Daniel traded his time of fellowship with the right people at the chapel for the wrong people at the bar. As he began to slip away from the moral virtues that his grandfather helped train into him, he started to notice health issues. Daniel tried to wait out the feelings of fatigue in hopes of getting better without medical attention, but he only got worse as time passed. The doctor diagnosed him with emphysema, which held serious implications for his health.

And for his military career.

He met with the medical board, which determined that he was no longer qualified to serve. The future that had looked so bright suddenly vanished in a fog of confusion. The floor gave way beneath Daniel's feet and he dropped into a cold, dark pit of despair. His hopes, his dreams, his future—the service to which he knew God had called him was suddenly being stripped from him. The news of his dismissal caused him to fall deeper into sin.

Feeling lost with no idea where to go next, Daniel knew it was time to get back home. Time to place his hand once more in the hand of his grandfather and find some direction. But the process of his discharge involved several months of transition time; he wasn't immediately "free to go." With his grandfather's health looking all the more bleak, Daniel's mom ended up submitting a request for emergency leave to the Red Cross. The Red Cross then informed the staff duty runner about the present condition of Daniel's grandfather, and the staff duty runner then informed his unit. Daniel would see his grandpa within a matter of days; or so he thought. A week passed before he received a written response that read, "Your emergency leave has been disapproved." The duty runner had mistakenly told Daniel's unit that a *friend*, not a family member, was passing away.

Hysterical, Daniel informed his commander of the mistake that caused his leave to be disapproved. The commander could do little. Daniel then wrote a letter to congress in hopes of getting quick help, but congress's response time was less than impressive. Daniel ended up having to submit the leave request through a different staff duty runner. The message was conveyed correctly the second time. The leave was finally approved after a long and frustrating month.

Grandpa was alive as Daniel flew home from Texas. Daniel stayed overnight in Portland to get some much needed sleep. Early the next morning he picked up a rental car and began his trip to Boise. Daniel was thankful to God that he would get one last chance to see the man who had made such a difference in his life.

But after one hour and forty-five minutes of driving, Daniel's cell phone rang. He pulled the car over to answer. It was his uncle.

"Hey, Daniel. Where are you right now?"

"I'm on my way to where you are."

"I need you to pull over."

"I already did. What's up?"

"Grandpa has passed away."

Daniel closed his eyes and bowed his head in broken sorrow; tears began to fall.

"But I'm almost there," he reasoned.

"I'm sorry, Daniel."

As he hung up the phone, bewilderment set in. Daniel's head spun dizzyingly. He tried to make sense of what he had just heard but the news was incomprehensible to him. Gradually he remembered that God is good. But if that's true, why couldn't God have waited a few more hours to take his grandpa? At least give Daniel the chance to say goodbye. Why would a good God let him come so close to seeing his grandpa alive only to smash his expectation and drop him into such a depth of sorrow?

Daniel turned his car around. He no longer had a reason to continue his journey to Boise. He ended up having to miss his grandpa's funeral, since his emergency leave was only approved for seven days. Angry and bitter, he flew back out to Texas to return to his post. Daniel would never be the same person after this experience.

In tragedies like these, it is hard to believe that a good and loving God can possibly exist. In the moments of despair we might justifiably question the nature of God. We might wonder if God is truly just and compassionate, as some believe Him to be. This type of questioning can become for some people a slippery slope into long-term bitterness. But when we can't see the answers to *why?*—when there seems no logical explanation for what God has done—we can continue to trust Him. When God seems cruel or indifferent, we can still trust that He cares. When God seems distant or weak, we can trust in His infinite power. And when God's choices seem foolish, we can trust that He is wise.

"My thoughts are not your thoughts, neither are your ways my ways, declares the LORD" (Isaiah 55:8). Much of the time we are unable to understand the purposes of God. *The reasons why God does what He does cannot always be seen by finite creatures, for they are often wisely and lovingly hidden by an infinite God.* After all, "Who has understood the mind of the LORD?" (Isaiah 40:13, NIV). Quite plainly, if God chooses not to explain, no one can understand His mind. He keeps things hidden and only reveals them *if* and *when* He wants to.

This is where faith, trust and patience come in. We walk a long journey in this life, and we sometimes trudge along under heavy burdens. God doesn't always explain His reasoning for giving us burden, but He has explained Himself—that He is in control, that He is all-wise, and that His love for us is perfect and infinite. If we endure and hold onto our confidence in God—in who He is, in His character—then we may be granted the blessing of seeing His purpose of allowing tragedy. Communicating what is within the depths of His heart and mind.

God's Artistry in Calamity

There are times when I have wished that I never had to experience calamity. I have wished that my parents never got divorced. I have wished that I could see my Uncle Joe again (he passed away in my youth). I have wished for many aches and losses to be removed from my life, believing that I would be better off never having known such sorrows. I think we all feel this way at times. We can wonder where God was when we needed Him most. Why He, in His power, would allow tragedy to have its natural way, breaking and embittering the spirit of man. I do not claim that I have all the answers, but I submit this story to you, illustrating one of the ways God allows and uses tragedy for good.

After eight years of marriage Joanne and I had a conversation about the critical events that had to occur in order for us to meet. We met at a foursquare church that was out in the boondocks, far out of the way for both of us. So how did we both end up there together? First, you have to understand that we were only seventeen, minors at the time, and many of the places we ended up going to were based on the choices of others. Next, my mom and dad had to divorce; otherwise my dad would have been attending a different church with my mom. Also, my dad had to make the hard choice of remaining at this church—the church whose pastor stole his second wife and led to his second divorce. Dad very much wanted to leave, but God said no. And one more piece to the puzzle: My depression was necessary to help me find God and to cause me to take any interest in attending His church with Dad. That's how I ended up there, because of a series of tragedies.

As for my wife, she also came to attend that church through the tragedies of others. Her dad has disintegrated discs in his back, which deter him and his wife from being able to attend church weekly; if his back were healthy, the family would have attended a church near them. Instead, my wife happened at the time to be dating the one boy in her area whose family would drive an hour out to the foursquare church every week. And the parents of her then-boyfriend would not have come to know God except for deep tragedies of their own, which I won't relate here.

As Joanne and I discussed all of this, I started to pick up on the common theme. The critical turning points that caused us to meet were not filled with joy and light. They were a series of dark, tragic events that no one saw coming. As we looked back on the history that brought us together, we saw the web of painful histories that ended up connecting us. I consider it one of God's miraculous ironies that He brought to me my wife—one of the greatest lights in my life and undoubtedly the greatest gift and blessing that I have on this earth—through tragedies, particularly the calamities of others.

Although God consciously allowed these sorrows, he has, at least in Joanne's and my case, birthed from them true love. Somehow God caused a piercing light to burst forth from deep darkness. I believe this happens—or could happen—more often than we recognize. How many people can look back and realize that some of their greatest gifts came, not through the joyfully momentous, but rather through the tragically painful? And please notice in my story that at least some of the turning points required a trusting response to God. If Dad had chosen not to listen to

God and stay at that foursquare church, or if I had chosen not to respond to God's intervention by going to church with Dad, Joanne and I would not have met. How many more blessings does God wish to birth from tragedy, if only we would trust Him in the midst of our pain? If only we would hold onto Him?

I hope that story helps you see what lies in the depths of God's heart and mind. In trusting Him, you will come to find that He is a redeeming God who can take the greatest of tragedies and bring out of them the greatest of blessings. He is a God who has the power to let tragedy move in and around our lives, and yet somehow delivers a beautiful outcome from those tragedies. He is like the artist who takes a painting that is filled with sorrow, and somehow arranges the final result so that the viewer sees the deep beauty in the whole.

This brings me back to Daniel. His story does not end in bitterness. Daniel was angry with God about his emphysema and the destruction of his dream. He was angry that he never got to hold his grandpa's hand. He was angry that he never got to mourn at his grandpa's funeral. He was *angry*. But his anger did not stop him from talking to God. In the midst of his tragedy, Daniel continued to seek an answer from his Lord and Savior. As he sought God his mind recalled Bible passages he had studied with his grandpa—passages like:

Beloved, do not be surprised at the fiery trial when it comes upon you to test you, as though something strange were happening to you. But rejoice insofar as you share Christ's sufferings, that you may also rejoice and be glad when his glory is revealed (1 Peter 4:12-13).

And

"Humble yourselves, therefore, under the mighty hand of God so that at the proper time he may exalt you, casting all your anxieties on him, because he cares for you" (1 Peter 5:6-7).

Months after his grandpa passed, Daniel and I talked late one night on the phone. He spilled his guts to me. We talked about his anger toward God and some of the things he had done because of that anger. He regretted the wrongs and repented before God. Daniel did what his grandpa trained him to do if he ever got lost: Go back to God.

Within weeks after that conversation I got another call.

"Hey, Josh."

"Hey, buddy."

"Josh, I have been giving a lot of thought to what I should do when I get out of the military." I figured that he would say that he wanted to do something in the medical field, but he threw me a curve ball. "I feel called to ministry. Youth ministry in particular."

My heart leapt as I saw a beacon of light coming out of Daniel's tragedy. Could it be that God allowed him to develop emphysema so that he could be removed from the army and called into ministry? And could it be that God allowed my friend to lose his grandfather tragically, knowing that it would help him turn back to his Savior? Daniel and I both agree that that is a very real possibility.

What do you think?

It Doesn't Always Work Out That Way

All this talk of light coming out of tragedy sounds pretty good in a book. But the Cinderella story that one would hope to see at the end of one's own tragedy may never come. Not in a recognizable form, at least. I am sure that plenty of times the good in a tragedy is and has remained completely unseen to the hurting. One can hope for good, and I believe that for God's children good will always come out of tragedy in some way, even if it is unseen (Romans 8:28). But we suffer nevertheless from day to day with the truth that we live in a corrupted world where an unmerciful evil exists.

It is not easy to live in this world, some days. Rarer and rarer are the days when I don't experience or hear about some sort of sadness—from a friend or family member or a quick glance at the TV news. That is why we need to walk ever so closely with God. Catastrophes and trials are around us all the time and so we seek a place of comfort and escape. If your first resort is solace in the things of this world, then you should know that the peace and comfort that this world offers, is nothing more than the peace and comfort that this world can offer. (Think about it.) *It is a limited comfort, and compared to God's presence and blessings, an inferior comfort.* Those who seek the Lord find a superior comfort—a comfort we gain when we choose to lovingly trust Him. Even in calamity.

Chapter 11

HOW DO YOU LOVE HIM?

—⟡—

"You will seek me and find me, when you seek me with all your heart."

—Jeremiah 29:13

I believe that humans having the ability to consider God is a profound evidence for God's existence. Think about it. As far as we know, we are the only creatures on earth that are capable of considering a thing as big as an Almighty Creator and Sustainer. I would have to argue that evolution makes no sense, since human beings are the only species that possess an ability to think philosophically, scientifically, politically. Not to mention all the other complexities of the universe that we ponder. Many scientists ascertain that there are millions of species that have existed for millions of years longer than humans, and yet none of them have once come within the same vicinity of intelligence as we have. Human beings are the only creatures capable of considering the worth of God. We are distinguished from the rest of the animal kingdom by our profound ability to search for God. And humanity's search for God is *the* most sought after revelation in human history.

We wonder about Him. We discuss Him in lectures. We read about Him in books. Some of us pray to Him daily in joyful fellowship. Others only pray to Him when times get rough, while still others do not pray to Him at all. We hear little children ask about Him and watch over little children who believe in Him. The child in all of us wonders if we will ever reach the far ends of space telescopically and see Him. We're unaware of a time when man did not search for God. Man wants to know whether or not God exists, and if He does, what He is like.

Why all this talk about our human capacity to contemplate God? Because only our human capacity allows us to *know* God. I'm not just talking about factual knowledge, although that's part of it. I'm talking, more importantly, about *personal, experiential knowledge of God.* I'm talking about a relationship.

God wants to be known. That's why He plastered evidence of His power and creativity all across the skies and the landscape (Psalm 19:1-6). That's why He sent Jesus, God the Son, in the flesh (John 1:1,14). That's why He gave us His written Word (John 19:7-10). And that's why He invites us, with open arms, to have faith in His Son and come boldly into His throne room— His very Presence—any time we want (Hebrews 4:14-16). The Almighty Creator wants to be known. And He wants to enjoy a personal relationship with you and with me.

Knowing God is the foundation of all other aspects of our relationship with Him. Paul acknowledged this when he wrote that in spite of his suffering and imprisonment, he was not ashamed to be associated with the Lord, "for I know whom I have believed, and I am convinced that he is able to guard until that Day what has been entrusted to me" (2 Timothy 1:12). The verb *know* is key in Paul's statement. He was saying, in other words, *I've become so well acquainted with God—I've seen and experienced His faithful love, His perfect wisdom, His infinite power—that no circumstances can shake my absolute confidence that He will be with me to the end.*

To know God is to *attain the basis* for complete trust in Him. To know God is to *see every reason* to love Him. To know God is to *establish steadfast resolve* in Him.

A Curious Word Called "Love"

Those who seek to know God ought to be envious of the apostle Peter. He literally walked with God. He watched God make known His kingdom to the world. Peter was one of the few in history who got to see God in the flesh (1 John 1:1-3). So you would think that Peter, by seeing such things, would have developed an unshakable resolve in the Lord. And indeed Peter demonstrated evidence of such confidence when he confessed Jesus to be the Messiah, the Son of the living God (Matthew 16:13-16). Jesus proceeded to play on Peter's nickname—"the Rock"—promising to build His church on the bedrock of Peter's confession (verse 18).

So what happened to Peter—the Rock who believed himself bound by steel to his Savior? The night of Jesus' arrest and trial, the Rock crumbled and denied his Lord three times, and he realized that his resolve to follow Jesus was not as deep as he thought.

Peter may have known the Lord better than anyone in history. He certainly knew Jesus better than most. But when trouble arose, his faith in his Friend and Savior failed. I wonder how many men have gone through the same type of scenario: They are sure within themselves of their faith in God, until the dark storm rises up to reveal their "faith" as mere pride, confidence in self, a house of cards. None of us has reached the point where we can say, "I have enough faith now." Like Peter, we're all in need of more faith as fallen creatures in a fallen world.

After His resurrection, Jesus knew that Peter's confidence had been severely shaken—perhaps to the point of no recovery, if Jesus didn't take measures to repair it. So what did Jesus do? Did He give Peter the drill sergeant treatment—a swift kick in the rear and a severe scolding: "Have some faith, maggot!"? Or maybe He used denial—sweep the whole thing under the rug and just go back to being buddies. Or perhaps He played the motherly kindergarten teacher, smothering poor little Petey in hugs while bandaging up his skinned knees.

None of the above. And…a little bit of all of the above.

Jesus knew that relationship was at the root of Peter's recovery. And so, in hopes of restoring relationship, Jesus confronted Peter three times with the key question: "Simon, son of John, do you love me more than these?" Peter answered, three times, in the affirmative (John 21:15-17). I love how Jesus asked "Do you love Me?" three times, as it shows just how much He cares about the love between us and Him. At face value, His question seems simplistic, calling for a simplistic answer. I mean seriously, if Jesus came and asked you face to face if you loved Him, what would you say? I know that some men would say, "I don't love You, Jesus. Matter of fact, I hate You." But especially for those who have considered the life of Jesus and the suffering He endured to open wide the door of salvation to humanity, I would assume most would say, "I do love You, Jesus."

But what do you mean when you say that you *love* Jesus? Consider the word love a little more carefully. *Love* is a word ill-defined in the English language; our one English word fails to capture the many possible meanings of this complex idea. For instance, in Greek (the language that the New Testament was written in), the word *eros* (pronounced AIR-os) is sexual love. It is commonly experienced through lust or desire. A man desiring his wife would be a good example. This type of love, though it is intended by God to be enjoyed in purity, is also closely associated with sinful desires. We all know where lustful desires can end up going.

Another word for love in the Greek is *storge* (pronounced store-GAY), a type of family affection. An example of this love is seen in how one feels towards one's father, mother, sibling, uncle, aunt and so on. And yet another word for love in the Greek is *phileo* (pronounced fil-EH-owe). This type of love is best understood between siblings, but also between friends. The city of Philadelphia (*phileo* "love" + *adelphos* "brother") was actually named after this Greek word, as it is understood to be the "city of brotherly love."

Lastly, and most significantly, the Greek language provides one more word for love. It is *agape* (pronounced a-GAH-pay). *Agape* is the greatest of all the love words in the Greek. To *agape* means to love sacrificially. The pinnacle of *agape* comes when one gives one's life out of love. It is a love that, in its positive sense, is pure and perfect, able to conquer and remove the greatest of boundaries. It is the type of love that Jesus exhibited when He died for you and me.

I am teaching you the meanings of these love words for a reason. You see, anyone can *love* Jesus, but it is the *type* of love that truly makes a difference. Jesus got specific about the types of love when He asked Peter three times if Peter loved him. Jesus asked one time if Peter *phileo* loved him—a good, wholesome, important type of love for the Lord. But more significantly, Jesus asked Peter two times if he *agape* loved Him. *Agape* love is the pinnacle type of love that Christ has for us. And He desires that we have the same kind of love toward Him.

But let's be honest, it is not an easy thing to *agape* love Jesus. *Agape* love is not for timid people. *Agape* love requires sacrifice and bravery. Peter discovered this hard truth for himself. We know that Peter lived a life true to his confession of *agape* love for Jesus. Notable scholars agree that Peter was martyred, hung upside down upon a cross for the Savior he loved. The arrangement of his crucifixion was reportedly at Peter's own request, for Peter did not consider himself worthy enough to die the same way that Jesus did. The death that Peter died for his Savior was a demonstration of *agape* love. What is more, we recognize by Peter's expression of love that he had come to *know*—intimately, deeply, personally—the one in whom he'd placed his faith. To know Jesus is to love Him and perhaps even be willing to die for Him.

Love in Deed

I ask you now, what kind of love do you have for the Savior? Take a minute to ponder the question. Do your actions demonstrate the kind of love you hope and want to have for Him? We can ponder the many ways we *think* we love Jesus, along with the many things that we *believe* we would do for Jesus. But let's be straight about this, thinking about how much we love the Lord doesn't take much. Our thoughts are never really proven until the words of our mouth and the acts of our hands are tested. We are called to *agape* love the Lord without compromise, seeking always to do the good we know we ought to do for the Savior. *To love in deed, is love indeed.*

Let me be honest with you and say that it is easy for me to *write* about sacrifice and loving God with the best kind of love. But rest assured that I too am a man who is far from perfect. I fail frequently. Sometimes I hear God tell me plainly what He wants me to do. And I don't. Sometimes I hear Him tell me what *not* to do. And I still do it. There are times that God doesn't need to tell me what to do, as my conscience or my awareness of His Word tells me what is right. Yet still I fail.

I recall one event in particular: I had just finished my military basic training and Tech School. I was enjoying my first day at my new duty station, Travis Air Force Base. I sat outside Joanne's and my temporary living facility in a comfortable armchair. In peaceful bliss I soaked up the California sunshine. But after fifteen minutes, my time of relaxation was suddenly invaded.

No more than twenty yards from me, I heard a child start screaming bloody murder. My ear tuned in to the blood-curdling cries. The child sounded no older than maybe five or six. I was able to distinguish an irate parent's voice roaring and cursing over the screaming child. It was a domestic disturbance characterized by verbal abuse to say the least, and I would not have been surprised if physical abuse was involved as well. The gears started turning in my head. Since my military training was fresh, I started to ask myself, "What was I trained to do in this situation?" More than that, I also asked, "What would God expect me to do?"

Both answers caused me to lean toward stepping in or at least calling Security Forces. Such responses would have been wise, and I should have taken action. Instead I ended up taking my time, thinking about what I should do. *I bet someone else will call it in* , I thought. *I'm sure somebody will do something about this.* As I debated internally, I ended up convincing myself that I didn't need to do anything at all. I didn't even pray. I never saw Security Forces show up; neither did I see anyone intervene. I have no idea what happened to that screaming child. To this day I look back on that moment and wish that I had done something. I was too lazy, though, or maybe it was that I was too scared. Whatever my problem was I know at least this much: I was wrong.

I obviously didn't know my Lord well enough to trust or love Him in action, as well as in word and intention.

With one compromise, more compromise came naturally. About a year after that event I recall another time when my wife and I were driving home from a wedding on the Oregon coast. Along the way we spotted a minivan that was pulled off to the side of the road. A man was reaching into the minivan shaking his child in the baby seat with what looked like panic; the child looked unconscious. Joanne and I were both concerned.

Joanne piped up. "We should pull over and help them."

In all honesty, I can say that I felt the Holy Spirit's movement telling me to do the same. My heart thumped out of my chest like it usually does when God is telling me to do something. Once again I began to think the situation through…to rationalize. I figured, *I don't need to pull over. Someone else will take care of it.* I write sorrowfully as I say that I did exactly nothing to help. I left it for someone else to take care of. I don't know what happened to that baby. I hope in my heart that whatever was happening, everything ended up okay. I wish I could *know* that everything worked out fine, but I do not have that luxury. I was too stubborn to pull over and be the help that God wanted me to be. I now have to live with the thought that maybe that baby died because I was unwilling to pull over. The decisions that I made about the screaming child and the unconscious baby hang on me still.

We sometimes know clearly what to do in order to pour our lives out for the Savior by helping those in need. But actually pushing through and taking action is where the challenge really lies. We have to do more than merely speak love for God; we must act out the love and courage we believe we have in the Lord. Doing so will both demonstrate and further develop our resolve and dedication to God. In so living, we live out a testimony before the world—a testimony of God's active love for His creation.

There have been many other times when I did not respond to God's call, and I regret them all. I will never know what good could have come from being obedient to His voice. But God has used the regret to prod me forward in some new situations; He has encouraged me not to be as timid in response to His calling.

I had recently taken on a Youth Pastor position at Powell Valley Covenant Church when I felt a pull on my heart from the Lord to step out in faith again. A young man, only sixteen years old, had been killed in a tragic car accident. The kids in the community wanted to hold a prayer vigil for their friend. My pastor okayed the use of our parking lot for the ceremony.

The day of the vigil arrived, and I, with no plans to partici-pate, had just finished a church meeting and was walking out to my car to go home. I noticed the kids gathering in the parking lot. I didn't know any of them, or their dearly departed. As I passed by them I said a little prayer and made ready to spend some time at home with Joanne and my boys.

I was in my car driving with only twenty yards from the parking lot exit when I felt that pull on my heart and a voice saying to me, *Why don't you get out and spend some time with them?*

As in times before, I was strongly tempted to talk myself out of listening. I could have replied, *Lord, Joanne and the boys are waiting for me, and I haven't spent much time with them today.* But because of my past failures, I was now ready to respond in the affirmative to God's calling. I didn't want to, once again, deal with the regrets. I pulled in front of the church and put the car into park. I climbed out, put my keys in my pocket and walked toward the back parking lot to where the kids were. *Lord,* I prayed, *please don't let this be weird.*

It did feel weird at first, walking toward all those kids not knowing any of them or their departed friend. I felt like I had no reason to belong there other than God telling me to go. I could have been that unwelcome presence that people don't want around. In paranoid fashion, I thought that I might get yelled at or kicked out for being an invading stranger. As I joined the group, though, one of my old youth kids who had just graduated ran up to me and gave me a hug. She told me that she was glad I was there and that she missed me. The warm greeting was an encouragement to my heart and made me feel like I belonged at least a little bit. I joined the crowd that encircled the memorial site and stood silently, content to observe.

It just so happened that as I waited for the kids to start the service I was standing right behind one of the leaders. I heard him say quietly to one of his friends, "This feels weird, man. Shouldn't we have a pastor here for something like this?"

Coincidence? Without a pause, I took one step toward the kid and said, "I'm a pastor."

"Are you serious?"

The kid knew nothing of me or where I was from, but, astounded at the turn of events, he asked me if I would be willing to say something at the appropriate time. How could I say no? I stood in the background as the vigil began, and I watched and listened. The youth who had just lost their friend spoke about the times and stories that they cherished with their lost loved one. They talked about his generosity and love for others. They reminisced about how wild and fun he was at parties. They laughed about all the times they got high and drunk together. Many eyes filled with tears that night, including my own. So many wondering, with hurt and pain, why their friend was taken from them so unexpectedly. After the stories were finished and silence settled on the crowd, the kid leading the service looked to me. I prayed silently that I wouldn't say something stupid, overly religious or offensive to these kids. I asked the Holy Spirit to give me the right words. I was totally unprepared, and was counting on God to help me minister comfort to the hurting.

I told the kids that I wished I had known their friend, that I wished we'd had the chance to share what faith we had. I told them that it was my hope and prayer that he was in the eternal kingdom with God. I told them that if they are seeking comfort, the shallow things of this world can never come even close to the comfort that God can give them. I told them to continue to share love with each other, and that through that love, they would be able to honor the memory of their friend. I told them that it was hard, maybe even impossible, to make sense of tragedies like these, but nevertheless, God was there to help them along in their pain if they only sought Him. I even got to share the gospel with them, sharing God's love and the payment that Jesus Christ paid to be near them and with them in times like these.

I can honestly say that many of the words were not my own. But, you see, I didn't have to know the words; *I only needed to know God.* Knowing Him caused me to trust Him lovingly enough to obey and step out in faith. God helped me that night to have genuine faith, to recognize that I simply can't operate by myself. You see, that is the key to understanding all this. The key to truly being sons and daughters who chase after the Father. *Chasing Him helps us to know Him. Knowing Him helps us understand that we must rely on Him. Knowing Him helps us recognize our own weaknesses. And knowing Him gives us confident faith in Him—faith to believe in His power that brings hope, healing, restoration and obedience.*

Love and Hope

I'm grateful that my dad stuck around as I've grown up, because the time he and I spent together allowed me to get to know him. Especially after his spiritual turnaround, knowing Dad has been an amazing privilege. Because I know Dad, I love him deeply, and I know that he loves me. Because I know Dad, we share with each other the times of joy and sorrow and challenge at a deep, deep level. Because I know Dad, I respect and trust him as my hero, and I'm able to imitate his positive example. Because I know Dad, I get to experience hope, healing and restoration. None of this would be possible if I didn't know Dad.

And so it also goes as I learn to know God. As I grow in my knowledge of God, I'm seeing that everything about Him is loveable. I love Him more and more, and I know better and better that He loves me without fail. As my understanding of God increases, I trust at a deeper and deeper level to share with Him the times of joy and sorrow and challenge. Because I'm learning to know God, I'm starting to respect and rely upon Him as my ultimate Hero, seeking to imitate His perfect example of heroic love toward all.

None of this would be possible if I didn't know God.

When we have come to know God, we can have many hopes for living our life for God. As for me, I hope by the time I am old—rattered and tattered, falling apart and barely hanging on to the hinges of life—that my Bible will be right there by my side in the same condition from doing the ministry that God has called us to. Because I know Him, I hope that my heart will forever remain sealed in the love of Jesus Christ as He teaches me *daily* what it is to be *fully* devoted to Him. Because I know Him, I hope to live a life of change by being the man who walks a road of righteousness and obedience. To be a light in a world that is full of darkness and decay. To be a warning sign of caution to any who journey on a road that leads to broken darkness and eternal hell.

What are your hopes? If they are godly hopes, I am confident you will fulfill them if you learn to know God. If you chase fervently after your Father.

One day my friend, the time of this world will come to an end, and we will be left holding only the things of true value, godly value. Among the things we hold will be the testimony God has given us and the love that He allowed us to express toward Him and others. We must open our eyes to the opportunities that He is placing before us, step forward in confidence with the feet He has given us, grasp tightly with the hands He has cleansed for us and love generously with the heart that He is sanctifying within us. In doing so, we move from faith to faith (Romans 1:17) with demonstrations of love toward the God whom we are so blessed to know.

Chapter 12

LIVING IN A ONE-STAR UNIVERSE

I have heard many say that love is blind. I remember being blindly in love with my wife, Joanne, at one point. To prove my love to her, I once ate mud from a puddle that looked like it had been trampled on by a number of feet. I could have gotten insanely sick. Blind love can be a dangerous force that causes us to do a lot of nonsense.

But what about love that's *partly* blind? What if you were to walk around with blinders around your face that kept you from seeing outside a limited angle of view? Many of us live this way, figuratively speaking. We focus our "sight"—our attention, our efforts, our devotion—toward one object, never realizing the huge, wide variety of other opportunities all around us. We can easily be part-blind in our pursuit of a dream or a hope. I almost didn't marry Joanne at the age of twenty because I was in love with the idea of attaining success first. I almost didn't have my first son Christian at the age of twenty-four, as I desired to finish college first. I was experiencing "love" of a sort—a part-blind love and a desire for the dreams that I wanted for myself personally. Does that sound familiar?

My Dad also held a dream for himself. I wasn't joking when I told you earlier that he had an ability perform on stage and play the guitar. Many people believed he had the skill to go the distance if he really wanted to. As a young boy at the age of eight I remember waiting for Dad to come out of the dressing trailer and greet his fans. Men shook his hand in respect. Women waited patiently in line to get his autograph. Even little children were excited to meet him. They were thrilled at the chance to give high fives to the "big star" of the show. Dad enjoyed the attention. Little by little his head grew with pride, and so did his desire to become something more.

At home, he'd already fulfilled the dream of many men—a beautiful house, a supportive wife and four children who loved him. But that wasn't enough for him. He was becoming blind to the blessings he had and began desiring the things he didn't have. When I was four years old, Dad made plans to travel to Canada for three months in an attempt to hit it big in the music industry. Mom didn't like the idea one bit. She communicated in her own way that she wanted Dad to stay home, but he was uninterested in his wife's needs. He was a man with a dream. But little did he know that chasing his dream would lead him into a nightmare.

Dad took his trip to Canada and returned home an empty man. His plans to make it to the top fell short; the one sweet thing in his life started to go sour. In seeking his own ambitions, Dad communicated to Mom that he was more interested in himself than in his family. There had been a time when Dad was blindly in love with Mom. But as is natural for all, when you stop dreaming about the people you selflessly love and start dreaming about the things you selfishly desire, you will end up losing that which is more precious.

It is likely that every person on this earth has a dream of some sort. Hopes of a successful job, a loving family, secure wealth, high prestige and so forth. These dreams are all well and good for the most part. After all, they are a piece of what keeps the adventure in life. But when someone begins to believe that fulfilling their own dream is the key to contentment, they are doing nothing more than looking through a narrow lens.

For example, the desire of wealth is a narrow lens through which many observe—or think they observe—the world. Some may say, "If only I could have such and such an amount of money in my account, then I would be content with life." I have found, though, that wealth usually does not bring a person closer to contentment; rather, it fosters discontent. After achieving their financial goal and a little time passes, they end up feeling all the more empty, dazed and confused as to why they do not sense peace in their soul, even with a full bank account.

It's because their view of the world and eternity is so limited; they're missing so much.

To me, chasing after contentment in such a way is like chasing an elusive dream, or walking toward a mirage that promises cold drink in a parched land. Even if one were to reach their "dream," they are only allowed to live it for so many years under the sun. In chasing dreams and contentment, and making them our focus, we live contrary to the sound wisdom of Jesus: "Seek first the kingdom of God and His righteousness, and all these things will be added to you" (Matthew 6:33). In other words, Jesus says there *is* something worth chasing, far beyond what the world has to offer, and that thing is the kingdom of God. You see, when we seek the kingdom of God first, it is impossible to be satisfied looking through the narrow lens of life's vanities.

The kingdom of God is too large for any telescope to capture in one framed view. When we seek God's will and His vision for our lives first, we find in the midst of His will a dream of greater magnitude that goes far beyond our own comprehension. If you haven't noticed, some of the stories in this book that I have told you are meant in part to paint a picture, showing that the hopes we personally have for our own lives are not necessarily the hopes that God holds for our lives. God has given us the awesome power of choice, to determine for ourselves how we will live and what we will chase after. For this reason, we have to be wise enough to take time to step back from the narrow lens, look around in all directions and perhaps find a totally new view that God calls us to.

Allow me to paint a picture that requires your help. I recommend that you actually try this when you get a chance. Envision yourself standing outside beneath a clear night sky. Before looking up, close one eye and with the other eye look through a narrow tunnel made from your curled fingers. As you look up into the sky, adjust your "viewing tunnel" until you are only able to see one star through your tightened fist. This is your narrow lens. You focus in on that star, become infatuated with that star. You begin to think, *How could I make that star mine? What would I need to sacrifice?* This is an illustration of what people do at times. They "zero in" and infatuate themselves with their one star. That star could be called "money," "fame," "respect" or "retirement." (What would your star be named?)

Continuing our illustrative exercise, after focusing in on your star, slowly begin to open your fist up. Broaden your scope. Start to notice the beauty of the stars around your star. Free yourself from the obsession with your one star, to consider and appreciate the others. Take the fist away from your eye and open your other eye. The view is magnificent, isn't it? A kingdom of stars. A visualization of the panoramic beauty that God means for us to see when we've been limiting our perspective. God has provided a wide, vast kingdom that we are to live for, and yet many of us limit ourselves to living for just one thing. What a tragedy.

I ask you now, what are you living for? Please understand that I am not trying to make you assume that the things you are focusing on and the life you are living are wrong. I am only trying to get you to consider that perhaps you're missing something that God intends you to see and include in your pursuits. He has a full, wonderful kingdom filled with many stars worth chasing and He longs to take you by the hand and lead you to the ones He has chosen for you.

Charting a New Course

When we back away from our narrow lens and open our view to include all of the possibilities in God's kingdom, we may find that we need to chart a new course altogether. As you look along your life's intended trajectory, I encourage you to ask, What kind of person will I be at the end of all this? What difference will the path I seek to travel really make to myself, and even more than that, to others, and still more than that, to God?

Many of us hope to have made a difference by the end. Many ask the questions: When my day comes, how many people will attend my funeral? What will they say about me? What kind of legacy will I have left for the world?

You are even now providing partial answers to these questions—by the way you choose to live your life in this very moment and in all the moments that follow. I have heard it said that the nice guy finishes last, and with such saying, man is sadly encouraged to seek his own needs first. In many cases, this old adage may be true, but frankly, *we should not care about being the nice guy who finishes last, nor the bad guy who finishes first. Quite simply, we should just want to be the godly man who finishes strong.* We should be driven by a single-minded desire to live first and foremost for God. Opening ourselves to all the various avenues that He would have us tread. It is a matter of taking the map that we have carefully drawn out for our own life and handing it over to God, who will confirm whether or not we're walking His path. It is a matter of yielding to Him the course we have plotted for our own lives so that we can assuredly walk in the blessed path that God has drawn out for us.

It is not easy, letting go of this life and letting God take hold of our destination. A serious trust issue can come into play here. What if God takes us down a road that we don't want? What if God does not plan an easy road? What if the dreams we hold are the complete opposite of God's desire for us? The will of God for our lives can suddenly look dark. We may start to believe that if we choose God's way, we will have to move far backward before we can make any movement forward. But don't let the enemy fool you into continuing "forward" if it means a lifetime of mediocrity. Satan will use any strategy he thinks might keep you from seriously considering God's will for your life.

In truth, we do take a risk in reconsidering our life's direction, in opening our hearts and minds to God's direction. But it's a worthwhile risk, and any sacrifice we make in this life by letting go of our temporal worldview is, in reality, an investment in eternity. The missionary martyr Jim Elliot wrote in his journal, "He is no fool who gives away what he cannot keep, in order to gain what he cannot lose." It is worth giving our all for Christ, for in giving Him our all, we are given the opportunity not merely to live, but to thrive. And not just for a while, but forever. If you sacrificially live out God's plan for your life, you will realize this great truth: *You can never be anything more than what you already are in Christ; and what you are in Christ is far greater than what you are able to invent or imagine.*

In Christ, we become men who rightly lay out our priorities, men who lead our families in faith rather than fear. In Christ, we become men who stand out in the crowd, crying out for the rest of the world to come to God.

The Difference a Little Love Can Make

Going through the military, I had the opportunity to get to know a lot of fine men and women. I would occasionally meet a person who was only working for a paycheck, but most serve because they sense a higher calling. Not a higher calling by God necessarily (though much of the time that was the case), but a calling to contribute to something bigger than themselves. A more than significant portion of those serving in the military today can be described as "high caliber" people. For this reason, not many military personnel stand out from the rest, because in some way, pretty much every military person is a leader. The person you are about to read about is one of those few—he is rightly distinguished as a leader among leaders.

During my time in the service many people came to the chapel seeking to address a spiritual need. After the need was met, many of the individuals were quickly gone without any plans of returning. One officer in particular, however, did not come to the chapel to *get* something, but rather to *give* something. I never got to know this man on a personal level, but something in him clearly distinguished him from others. On the day I first met him I recall seeing on him a look of joy that few displayed. There was another airman sitting across from me, and as was custom we both rose to attention as he entered the office.

"At ease, airmen. Take a seat," he said. We did as he asked and waited to hear the officer's request. "How are you two doing today?"

"Fine, sir. How can we be of service today?"

"You can tell me how things are going for you. I just want to know how you are doing."

The other airman and I looked at each other a little confused. You see, no one really came into the chapel to see how the chapel staff were doing. It was commonly assumed that anyone working in the chapel had no needs, that everything must be perfectly fine in our lives since we were "working for God."

The officer went on to ask more questions—where we were from, why we joined the military, and so on. As we each explained a piece of our story, we could tell from the way he listened that he really did want to know who we were and how we were doing. I worked active duty in the military for four years and never met anyone outside the chapel who cared like this man did. After talking for a bit, the officer let us know that he would be back to check on us again. He was true to his word. He must have visited another five times before he was due for retirement.

I appreciated his visits, looked forward to his visits; they lightened my day a bit each time he came in. This is one reason that this man stuck out to me as a leader. I didn't know a thing about his background, but I was encouraged by the type of man he was and the way he genuinely cared for me and for others. He made a difference in the lives of many people because he was clearly open to and following God's plan for him; he wasn't limited to some narrow view of his life's purpose. And his example caused me to ask myself if I was able to be so open, to love people the same way he did. After all, God calls all of us to genuinely love and care for others; it's part of His plan for everyone. And, in fact, I would argue that the greatest power on earth is love and that through love both the least and the greatest of people can make a positive impact. As stated by Mother Teresa, "Not all of us can do great things. But we can do small things with great love."

It Is My Faith That Defines Me

This outstanding man's story includes one more detail I want to communicate to you. He would frequently repeat a particular saying. And for him it was more than mere words; he lived by it: "It is my faith that defines me." As he neared retirement, he repeated his slogan more and more often, and the way he used the words and looked at people when he said it, you could tell that he was trying to get across a specific point. He never directly said what he meant by the quote, but the more you got to know him, the more you could understand what he was hoping to communicate.

Because of his faith, he was a man who clearly showed love to all. Because of his faith, his face often displayed a look of joy layered with contentment. Because of his faith, he had no fear of showing love and affection toward his family, even in public. The point? As an officer, he had to abide by many military laws, but it was clear that he had opened his vision to include more than a narrow focus on things military. He recognized his calling to an even higher law. More than the leader who can be bred by the *military* standard—a worldly type of standard—this man was a leader bred by *God's* standard.

How does a person get to such a place of profound interpersonal impact and leadership? "It is my faith that defines me," he would say... On the day of his retirement, this man painted a verbal picture for his audience so that we might understand more clearly what he meant when he spoke of "faith" defining him. He told the story of his life at home as a boy and how it was *God* who helped direct his young life. He spoke of his life in the military and how *God* directed him to join the service. He spoke of his life as a family man and how he depended on *God* to help him be the man that he needed to be for them. As we all listened, he made it clear that his life was directed with purpose—not a purpose directed by his own hands, but a purpose directed by *God's* hands. He spoke of his love and affection for the Savior, which helped him through the hardest parts of life. And I think everyone knew which Savior he was talking about.

It was this man's faith in Jesus Christ that defined him, and to Jesus Christ he always looked first for answers. He counted on God's leading; he became a man who did not seek his own kingdom, but God's kingdom. He could be branded in the world's eyes as successful and lucky beyond measure, but he was much more than that; he sought for the high treasure of being a godly man who could carry his wealth of love on to eternity. In this life, we'll never know exactly what difference a life like that makes. But this man's life changed me, and what he stood for will stay with me forever. I know that others feel the same way about him. By his very existence and example, he causes others to ponder whether they're walking the right path themselves, for the right reason.

Are you willing to make this kind of difference in others? You can. But you'll need to live with your eyes wide open, willing to set aside your few and narrow goals and dreams, willing to see the breadth and depth of God's amazing kingdom and follow His path along the road you are meant to travel. We're all travelers, but few travel knowingly according to an intentional plan, and even fewer a plan intended for them by their Creator. Many fix their eyes so firmly down on the next step or two that they never look up or think of the end, the destination; they may as well be living on a treadmill. There are some, however, that are so fixed on the road that leads to eternity, *a road filled with light,* that it makes clear the walking path of life from beginning to end. They know exactly where their path leads because it is God who leads them to the gateway of heaven. They look ahead with expectation in their hearts and gaze upon the gates of pearl that they will one day enter.

This is absolute love. And it's certainly not blind.

Chapter 13

THE CONSEQUENCES OF SIN VERSUS THE CONSEQUENCES OF CONFESSION

We've joked about being blinded by love. And we've talked more seriously about being part-blinded by a narrow, obsessed focus on a personal dream. It's time now to talk about something with the insidious power to blind completely and destructively. Sin.

Sin has a way of clawing into our lives and slapping our faces sideways. Our gaze is suddenly slapped away from our focus on God, and the ironic thing is, we think the slap feels good. Sin in the body can be like a tasty treat. Little do we recognize ourselves as the little mouse walking into a huge, baited trap, and sin is the cheese. You know what happens next!

I sometimes indulge in wishful thinking, wishing I could lessen the consequences of sin. When I really want to sin, I sometimes try to convince myself that the repercussions will not be too dire. In the end, though, I find the words of Jesus' brother James to be all the more true when he says, "Each person is tempted when he is lured and enticed by his own desire. Then desire when it has conceived gives birth to sin, and sin when it is fully grown brings forth death" (James 1:14-15).

Many people turn their lives for the worse, consuming themselves in drugs, pornography, fornication, alcohol and money. The list could go on and on about the carnal idols to whom so many men and women have devoted their lives. Countless people have lost their physical and spiritual life to these addictive substances and habits. Sin is dangerous! That's a no-brainer for anyone with an ounce of wisdom. But such wisdom is a rare commodity these days, because sin makes you stupid.

It is stupid to throw away a seasoned marriage for a one-night stand. It is stupid to fill your body and life with drugs and alcohol, causing you to lose your grip on reality and dive deeper into the trenches of death and darkness. It is stupid to get on the computer and look at pornography, wasting your time, focus and energy on a moment's gratification. It is stupid to fantasize about the life you do not have, forgetting to give thanks for the life you do have.

Just take a look around you. Observable reality abounds with evidence of the foolishness of sin, but it can be so enticing in the moment of desire. It makes the road of eternity appear vague, fading into the background. How tragic to lose focus even for a moment on the kingdom to which we are called. We know the kingdom of God far exceeds the kingdom of sin in every measure. But our temporal view of this world can so easily draw us away from the eternal view. Draw us down…into death.

Other Things at Stake

Death is the greatest and final consequence of sin, but it is still only one consequence of many. Though we have an idea in our minds and a hope in our hearts for the person that we desire to be, the power of sin keeps us from what we truly need, which then keeps us from who we truly want to become. The ways we invest our time can make all the difference. Having some years under my belt as a believer, I notice a difference in my mood and in my spirit when I neglect Scripture. I notice a perspective change and a mood change when I have not taken as much time to read God's Word. D.L. Moody said, concerning Scripture, "Either this book will keep me from sin, or sin will keep me from this book." I also notice that when I don't spend time in prayer, I begin to lose my sense of compassion for others. Prayer is an opportunity to seriously consider the suffering of those near and far. Prayer can lead you to loving God and others on a deeper level. I've also noticed that when I stop going to church, I feel spiritually empty.

Your experience might not be exactly the same as mine, but we all need the same spiritual nutrients—the same *spiritual disciplines.* And when we fail to practice these habits we miss out on more than we realize. We have been blessed by God with the opportunity to draw closer to Him; He has equipped us with all we need for this purpose, but whether or not we take advantage of this opportunity is entirely up to us. You are not forced to read Scripture, but you miss out on its transforming power when you neglect it. You are not forced to pray, but you miss out on a deeper intimacy with God when you choose to not turn your eyes and ears toward Him. You are not forced to go to church, but you miss out on communing with other saints, the very ones with whom you will also fellowship in heaven. Indeed, there is much more at stake than death alone when we choose to allow sin to have power over us, when we neglect the deeper disciplines in our walk with God. How blessed is the life that we have the opportunity to live, if only we would flee from sin and yield ourselves to the Lord.

Too Many Good-Looking Girls, Man

Each of us usually has one particular spiritual battlefield on which sin can take a real hold on the soul. We're all guilty of plenty of sins, but I'm talking about that sin that really grabs hold of you. For me, it's failure to maintain sexual purity. Books and books have been written on this particular topic. It is an issue that has carried over through the ages with man (and woman as well), and will continue with us until the day we have crossed the line into eternity. I have heard it said that "99 percent of guys struggle with this issue, and the other 1 percent lie about it."

Once, as a young man, I tried to tackle this issue head on. I have found that when you try and keep a sin in the closet, it has a significantly greater chance of becoming a deeper issue that can rule over you. So I thought it good to gather some other men around me who would be an encouragement in dealing with this sin. One man in particular at my church was reputed to be a prayer warrior and an elder of sorts. He displayed a fire and passion for God in his worship, and seemed to be a man who put the things of God first. He was the guy to whom I had decided to go and open up about my struggle. I figured, if anyone has some wisdom or encouragement on this issue, it would be him. Following a Sunday service, I discreetly went to this gentleman to tell him my struggles and hopes of getting this particular sin under control.

After I let everything out, the guy put his hands on both my shoulders, looked me straight in the eye and said to me, "Son, there are just some issues that can't be overcome, and sometimes the better thing to do, is do nothing at all."

He elaborated further, telling me that it was okay to have this kind of sin. He said that every guy has this problem, so why not me? I honestly didn't know what to think. At the time, I didn't know much Bible and I assumed this guy did, and here he was telling me to just go on sinning and not have a care in the world about it! At the time I thought, *Maybe he's right. There are just too many good-looking girls, man. Too much distraction.* I thought of Job, who made a covenant with his eyes to not look upon a young woman with lust (Job 31:1). But young women in his days wore nonrevealing robes.

I began to question whether or not I should even try to establish the same kind of covenant as Job did. My young mind started to believe what "the man of God" was saying. From the counsel of that man, something very dangerous was birthed inside me. My deep desire to be pure was smothered a bit that day. A man that I believed was chasing after God had thoroughly confused me on one of the most intense topics of life, and there I stood, confused about how I should deal with sexual sin.

No doubt, keeping one's eyes and mind pure has become harder in today's age. Advertising and Hollywood constantly look for ways to stimulate our minds in their programming, and the common consensus between the two has been that sex will get the job done. The world sells sex as the pinnacle experience for mankind. It tells you daily, "Why not go out and have your fill? Put your trust in your hormones while they are still going wild in you. After all, you only live once, so you'd better live it right!"

Oh, how dangerous is this misuse of sex. The world has perverted one of God's greatest gifts. Sex, the blessing that has sustained humanity upon the earth. Sex, the abuse of which has taken countless souls to their physical and spiritual deathbeds.

Getting a Little More Personal

Sexual impurity nearly led me down the path of death—death of a potential marriage, death of my dreams, death of a life that could have been invested in everything right. Though Joanne is the only woman that I have ever known, I still hold a deep regret from years past. Before marriage, Joanne and I had sex. God did his best to keep us from making that mistake. As a matter of fact, there was a time when two random dogs came walking in on Joanne and me when things were getting a little too heavy. Before getting into our wild kissing session, Joanne and I had made sure that no one was around before locking up the house so that we could keep our sinful pleasures hidden away. We began to play our kissing games that would lead to the land of trouble. Just as things were clearly beginning to go too far, in walked two dogs out of nowhere. I mean nowhere. The house had been checked and rechecked to make sure no living presence was around. And I am *still* very certain that I securely closed and locked the door to the bedroom we were in. But still, in walked these dogs. One dog was black and the other was white. They looked like small Alaskan huskies—not really the type of dogs that could break down a door. In they came, though, to interrupt a game that promised to become very physical. I remember the dogs looking up at us with a peculiar look, as though asking, What are you guys up to? It freaked both of us out and quickly ruined the mood.

The dogs were friendly, so we walked them around the neighborhood in search for the owner. After knocking on some nearby doors, we found the owners about two blocks away. They were puzzled as to how the dogs got out, since their gate was still latched shut. "First time that's ever happened," they said. We still don't know how those dogs got in, other than God teleporting them there. Joanne and I both consider that event a miraculous intervention that kept us from premarital relations that day. Yet even after that event we eventually fell. Now, you might be saying at this point, "So you had sex outside of marriage. Big deal. Welcome to the large majority of the population on planet earth." It *is* a big deal, though. The people we choose to invest in and give ourselves over to make the deepest of impacts. The timing of giving ourselves over is equally important. When we had sex, I gave myself to Joanne, and Joanne gave herself to me.

Problem was, at that time there was only one person to whom I was supposed to be giving myself over, and that was God.

How great a division—a barrier—I created between myself and God on the day that I chose to fall. Though I did not feel like I was doing so in that moment, I was blatantly rejecting God in my life, telling him I would rather have the touch of a woman than His touch. My shallowness was made manifest in my lack of self control and in my true desire. Yes, I wanted God, but I made it clear in my actions that I wanted Joanne more. My rejection of God was sheer destruction that I invited into my life, and the destruction went further. Joanne had believed that I sought to be a man of God first, but after our sin, in her mind I was revealed as someone or something other than she had thought. After that, Joanne saw me as a man of compromise, and rightly so. I still wish that I could take that day back. Though God in his grace has restored Joanne and me, I still wish I'd never made that decision; it led to other problems later—particularly problems for Joanne placing her trust in me.

We Need Our Women to Believe

"Why don't you trust me?"

Have you ever asked this question of anyone? I know that I have asked Joanne that question more than once. And when I *really* think about the question, I'm able to come up with some pretty good answers myself. For one, I am a fallible man, capable of great evil, regardless of what others may think of me. I am convinced that any good that comes from me comes from God first. I am prone to sin, a depraved human being, just as depraved as the man or woman next to me on the street. If you are honest with yourself, you will likely admit that you have the same kind of humanity as I.

Sin is no stranger to any man. We need help from day to day to continue the good fight, seeking God's will for our lives. We all need help, someone to come alongside us and lift us up out of the trenches that we are sure to fall into. That is who Joanne has been for me in many cases, but not all. I can't tell you how much it means to me when my wife communicates the things she does or does not believe about me. What she believes about me can mean the difference between a good day and a bad one. It can mean the difference between a good decision or a bad decision. What Joanne believes and says about me can either encourage or discourage me as a man. Though I try to look to God first as my encourager, the words of my wife also hold a significant amount of power.

There are times that I *need* her to believe in me. Times that I *need* to hear her sing a praise or two about the good I have done her as a man. I need to know that she loves me for who I am, and even more, loves me for who I am trying to become. But before she can do that, I have to be a man who is seeking to become something better. I have to demonstrate what kind of man I am hoping to become, for God and for her. I lost a lot of trust with Joanne on the day that we fell out of purity. I proved to her that I am a man of compromise and sin, a man who does not always do the right thing. I had to reearn her trust by demonstrating my commitment to making the right choices. Rather than ask her if she trusts me, maybe I should ask myself first, "*Should* she trust me?"

I mean, seriously, look how we, the men, have treated our women. In many cases, women have become nothing more than objects for our gratification. Our culture has done a near flawless job of telling our women that their value is only found in their physical beauty. Many women have come to believe now that being a mother, and a mother only, is a worthless occupation. That is one reason why so many women are seeking out business careers. They want to feel as though they are doing something significant, something valuable. The truth of the matter is that, regardless of what women do, women are invaluable—we men just fail to tell them so. We also fail to tell them that they are beautiful, even if they are a bit overweight. We fail to value their words, especially when we consider that our women's words might be the very wisdom that God wants us to hear, spoken through the Holy Spirit. We fail to stand up as the men of God that we are called to be, allowing insults to be hurled upon our women, not only by the world, but also by us, the very ones who are supposed to defend our women.

We need our women to believe that we can be something more than what we have been. But such a belief starts with us and our actions; our leadership. You see, men, we are not called to follow our women to church; we are called to lead our women to church. We are not called to watch our women desire men in romance novels; we are called to be twice the men that our women read about in romance novels, godly men. We are not called to sleep around with multiple women; we are called, each man, to bring his woman into the presence of God and give her rest. We are called to inspire our women to holiness by living holy lives ourselves. From the beginning, God has established us as protectors of His beautiful creation. We are supposed to take that creation by the hand and lovingly lead her to God's throne.

That is what a trustworthy man will do. Are you a man who can be trusted?

One Example of Such a Man

I've told you about the valuable inspiration that my father brought into my life in my teen years. Still today, years later, he is capable of the same kind of inspiration. I have benefited from many conversations with my dad. Sometimes we just get together for lunch and talk about life. He speaks to me with an honest and open heart about his successes and failures. I treasure his words as he shares godly wisdom that helps navigate the direction of my life. There are many lessons that stick, but some lessons go beyond sticking. Some lessons become ingrained within my soul—lessons that Dad does not present in word; they are lessons he presents in action.

For many years now, my dad has continued to try his hardest to be a son who chases his heavenly Father. His pride is not what it once was (but he is confident). The love that he has for his wife is a love centered on Christ (the kind of love every woman hopes for). He continues to worship before the Lord musically, using his gifting with voice and guitar to inspire others to worship. But even more influential than all of that, he simply seeks to live a life of noble intention before his God. He has provably, demonstrably become the new man that Paul refers to in the New Testament. And this has happened not just in one day, but over thousands of days of faithfulness and dedication to the Savior. He is not a perfect man, but he consistently seeks to become perfect as he allows God to shape his heart and guide his life.

It was a weekday evening, just like any other. After putting my boys to bed, I turned on the TV for some time to relax. It was around nine thirty when my cell phone rang. I looked at the phone's screen to see who was calling. It was Dad. I thought about ignoring the call, but Dad never called late at night. It had to be important. I turned off the television and answered.

"Hey, Dad."

"Hey, son."

Dad took time to ask how his grandsons and daughter-in-law were doing. He asked me if life and work were going well. "Everything is great Dad" I said to him. But I could sense that Dad was calling to do more than inquire about work and family. I enjoyed the conversation, waiting for him to tell me his ultimate purpose. Finally, Dad paused for a moment. I waited silently to give him room to say what he needed to.

"I've been meaning to talk with you about something, son."

"Okay, Dad."

Another short pause ensued.

"I want you to know that everything in my life is going okay right now, but I have come to some major decisions as of late." I could hear the sincerity in his voice, and I recognized that he was trying to address a serious issue. "For years now I have been struggling with purity. I'm not having an affair or anything, but I continue to fall in ways that I don't want to. I keep on thinking about getting this sin into the light, but I have convinced myself for many years as to why I shouldn't."

The sin Dad was talking about was accessed through his computer screen. He'd made it his mistress, if you know what I mean...the same adulteress to whom many men, including myself, have gone. Dad was confessing his heart to me. At first I didn't know what to think. I just listened, ever so silently weighing the magnitude of what I was hearing.

"I'm tired of this issue owning me," Dad continued. "I'm tired of it tainting my marriage with poison. I'm tired of not loving my wife and honoring God the way that I am supposed to."

He went on to tell me about how he'd opened up to even his wife and his pastor on this issue. And I'm telling you, that's not easy. The man was taking some bold and courageous steps. The kind of steps that many other men would never dare to take. My heart swelled up as Dad laid his out before me. My dad was already a great man. And that brave phone call made him even greater. He was stepping out into an entirely new realm of faith. In essence he was telling me, "I still don't have it figured out completely, but I'm doing my best over here and I'm calling to let you know what kind of efforts I plan to make." As he told me more of his decision to battle for purity, the adage, "Like father, like son," haunted my mind. I thought to myself, *My father is battling for purity, even after so many years, and it is a battle that I fight, and lose, too.* It felt like Dad was in my corner all of a sudden, telling me of his own struggles, but implying, *I know that this beast can be defeated.*

The battle for sexual purity is against a beastlike foe, perhaps one of the greatest of all beasts. It seems unconquerable at times, especially when you are trying to fight it on your own. But perspective changes when other men come alongside you and say, "I'm fighting the same battle. Let's see if we can't take it on together, and take this monster out with the help of Christ!" That is the kind of man that I am talking about. The kind of man whom God uses. The type of husband who proves to his wife that he is running toward, not away from, God. The type of father who inspires his son.

I have sometimes wondered why Dad opened up to me that night about his struggle for purity. He could have decided never to tell me about it. But had he done that, a new dimension of our relationship would never have existed. My dad and I now talk openly and regularly about sexual purity. We encourage each other, pray with each other, understand each other. In all honesty, I don't even remember having the old birds-and-bees talk with the old man when I was young, but now we have talks that go much deeper than birds and bees. We talk in depth about what it means to live as honorable men, men who just might be able to defeat a great dragon together.

I trust my dad's word now. I didn't always do that. He had to earn my trust. And as time has gone on, he has proven himself through word and deed. He is, and yet is also becoming, the new breed of man that this world needs. He is trying to die daily, living like the man who said, "I have been crucified with Christ. It is no longer I who live, but Christ who lives in me. And the life I now live in the flesh I live by faith in the Son of God, who loved me and gave himself for me" (Galatians 2:19-20).

Chapter 14

WHAT WILL YOU SEE?

——∞——

Death. We all must face that fearsome and final foe some day. George Bernard Shaw wisely said, "The statistics for death are quite impressive—one out of one people die." It's not optional. In light of this—in the remaining years of preparation for final death—we do well to address the real question: Am I going to devote myself to living the life *I* want to live, or am I going to devote myself to daily dying the death God wants me to die?

When I was a little boy, I used the threat of death to try and leverage my Mom's will. I used to try the age-old trick of holding my breath to get what I wanted. I never tried it on Dad, but Mom was another story. I remember one night when she was cooking asparagus, I had never eaten this strange vegetable before; and after looking at it neither did I plan to eat it that night. The only vegetable I wanted was tomato sauce on my pizza.

First, I lightly walked over as cute as could be to my mother by the stove and gently tapped on her shoulder to get her attention.

"Yes sweetheart?" my mother said.

I spoke in the soft and cute voice that every mother loves to hear. "What're you cookin'?"

"Asparagus, sweetheart."

"I don't think I want that. Can we have pizza instead?"

"What I'm cooking is the thing you are going to eat."

She looked down at me intently as she said it, making sure our eyes connected. I knew exactly what she was saying; I had seen that look in Mom's eyes before. It is the look of mothers everywhere that says they mean business. To me, as a little boy, she was declaring war.

I burst out in a scream with no warning, "There is no way that I am going to eat that!"

Mom responded by rolling her eyes away from me to the frying pan and just went on cooking. I took a deep breath and held it in. I held it for a good ten seconds before frustratingly tapping her shoulder to make her aware of this new threat. She was already quite aware, though, and looked down at me with a smile.

I exhaled with fury and yelled, "What do you think is so funny? I'm going to kill myself if you don't get me some pizza!"

At that point she started to laugh. It was quite obvious that Mom understood my chances of death a lot better than I did. I tried to hold my breath another three or four times, but I discovered that, unless I taped over my mouth and nose holes, I was going to keep on breathing naturally. Oh, how greatly I strained my will that night against Mom, but it all ended with me eating her asparagus, not my pizza. I warred with my mother for a good hour over that vegetable; it was an hour of lasting significance. When I look back on that event now, I am glad that Mom stood firm. I know plenty of mothers who would have succumbed to a tantrum like mine and given their child their precious pizza (or whatever it is that they wanted).

I did not want my vegetables, but Mom, with wisdom far exceeding my own, knew that I needed my vegetables, even if I thought they were going to kill me. I threatened my bodily death, but something else died instead. I think a piece of my stubborn will died that night, thanks to Mom. That is what we need from our authorities—a purposeful resolve to do the right thing. Without the help, guidance and protection of another's good will in our lives, we may find very quickly that we are walking toward the cliff edge—with every intention of falling off.

A Cross to Bear

I demanded pizza from my mother. In similar fashion countless men have asked or demanded their life's desires of God. Little do we know, God is cooking up something greater than we could ever want for ourselves. Like every loving parent, God has a hope, perhaps you could even call it a dream, for our lives. He sees the treasures of greater value that we can gain; he sees the greater person that we can become. But to become that person, God must give us what we need, not what we want.

What if on one fine day, God came to you and offered you a magic card that guaranteed you could have any request you desired for the rest of your life. Would you take it? Before answering, consider this verse: "What does it profit a man if he gains the whole world and loses or forfeits himself?" (Luke 9:25). You see, if we were to gain the desires of our own hearts, hearts that are deceitfully wicked (Jeremiah 17:9), we would find that our own desires would likely consume the humanity that God has placed within us. When you get what you want, you become like a spoiled brat. I have met forty-year-old brats in my lifetime (some even older).

Those who are growing in maturity focus not on the things they want for themselves, but the object that God appoints for us to carry from day to day. It is not a thing that we would likely choose for ourselves, but we are called to pick it up and carry it anyway. It is a *heavy* and *burdensome* thing, an instrument of torture and death, and when carried correctly it feels both weighty and fulfilling. It is the cross, your cross. One might ask, though, "Where is my cross?" or "What is my cross?" Well, my friend, that is between you and God. I can tell you this much at least: It is not the kind that some people wear on chains around their necks. No, it is a cross that comes much closer to your heart than just the skin of your chest. It is the cross that Christ has called you to carry, and not for your destruction, but for your benefit. It is a cross that some have not even moved an inch, but if they did move it, they would feel a sweet release from the chains and bondage of their own desires.

The cross is meant to produce agony and anguish, and it is in your agony and anguish that you learn a new discipline. You discover the great worth of a life lived for more than self. You begin to die to your fleshly self, and allow the Spirit of God to cultivate His new life within you. That is the type of death that God desires for you to die. It is a scary death when seen in the flesh, but a beautiful death when seen through the Spirit. It is the death that God wishes for us all, for it is the very death that will bring us closer to Him.

My First Miracle

Death threatened my life during my first days in this world. As a young baby at the age of ten days, I came down with a fever. My temperature got up as high as 101.2 degrees, a temperature that is *very* dangerous for a newborn. Mom rushed me to the hospital emergency room where I was assessed by the pediatric doctors. The doctors decided to place me on an IV for fluids, along with three days of antibiotics. After three days' treatment, they still saw no major improvement in my health. The doctors reassessed me and agreed that I may have had a meningitis infection. I was given a scalpual IV and had ampicillin administered in hopes of removing the possible infection. I was receiving a dose of ampicillin at least three times a day and each dosage was to be administered *slowly*.

One day, after my mom had fed me, the nurse entered the room to give me another dose of ampicillin. As a mother and a registered nurse, Mom stayed by my side much of the time and made sure that I was properly cared for. Mom watched the nurse inject the ampicillin, and she noticed that it was being injected too quickly.

"Stop!" she shouted. "You are pushing the medicine through too fast."

It was too late, though. The sudden overdose caused my body to start spasming. I went into a seizure and stopped breathing. Frantic, Mom ran out of the room and started screaming out for help. Three white coats came rushing in and began to try resuscitating me. Mom was removed from the room as the doctors worked. I can only imagine what was going on in her head. Two minutes passed, then three, four. Still no word of my revival. Things were looking more and more hopeless. After about five minutes, one of the pediatric nurses—a devout believer and a dear friend of my mom—stepped out of the room where the doctors were still trying to revive me. Mom feared that I was done for; her friend confirmed her fear.

Mom's friend came by her side and asked, "Would it be okay if I baptized your son?" She meant baptism by sprinkling, as some faith traditions practice it. She believed it would grant me entrance into God's kingdom, where my mom would see me again one day.

Mom considered the request and accepted. So the nurse went back in the room and sprinkled me with water. Only seconds after the simple ceremony, I began to breathe again on my own. Everyone in the room could hardly believe what they had just seen. Upon checking my vitals, the doctors and nurses also discovered that my fever had disappeared.

After I returned to life, the doctors told my mom, "Well, he's breathing, but with the length of time he went with no oxygen, and the fever, he is likely going to have some developmental issues." That should have been the case. After everything that happened, I could have been a vegetable for the rest of my life. As time went on though, Mom and Dad watched their little infant develop along a normal scale of progression.

All of this happened on Easter Sunday morning of all days. Coincidence? I believe God saved me that day. He could have taken me into His heavenly kingdom so many years ago, but He determined that my time had not yet come. By all human expectations, I shouldn't be typing a single word in this book, but it is God who determines the length of our time on this earth. It is a limited time that will one day lead into limitless time. And until that day, the day we cross over into eternity, we make an impact on this world.

What impact will you leave on this world? There will come a time in your life when you will have to look back on everything you've done. On the day that you turn your gaze to the past and look down the road of life you've traveled, what will you see? Will it be a path of cluttered and haphazard destruction? Or will it be a path of purpose and beauty? And keep in mind that the road you will have laid out is one that small and tender feet will tread right behind you. Our past is a significant part of our children's future. And there is no greater future we can hand over to our children than an eternal future in Jesus Christ.

With these thoughts in mind, I've written three letters, which follow. If you have not placed your faith yet in Jesus Christ as your Savior, then the first letter is addressed to you. If you *are* already a believer in Jesus, then the second letter is addressed to you. And I invite you, in either case, to read the third—an open letter to my father.

A Letter to You Who Are Considering Jesus Christ

Dear friend,

Your life is like a house, and it has a door. Right now that door stands closed, and Someone on the other side is waiting for you to open it. Whether or not this door will be opened to this hopeful guest is up to you because He is a gentleman who will not barge in through a closed door. He stands patiently outside your door waiting for you to open it. You express your invitation to Him by opening the door. We call this step "faith." And when you open up to Him, He will faithfully enter.

This Man has always been standing at your door in hopes that you will give Him the chance to trust His entry into your life. He wants to meet you where you are right now, sin and all. Upon entering, He will begin to eradicate all that is evil in you and to replace it with His light. He is a man of unwavering truth. A man who carries hope into the places He goes. He is a man who offers forgiveness to the offender, and compassion to the afflicted. He is generous in His giving, to the point that He cannot be outgiven. He takes us by the hand and raises us, the crippled, out of the trenches. Strength can be felt in His hands and love can be seen in His eyes. He is a lover of all men, but detests the sin within man. He knows His family, and loves His family. Even to the point of dying for His family. His name has stood strong against the testimony of skeptics. His ideals have stood solid throughout time. He holds a truth that is the answer to every man's struggle to find purpose. His name remains the most famous of names among men. Countless testimonies have been declared that, through His name alone, impossible healings and restorations have come. It is a name that many know now, and after time has ceased, all will know...

Jesus the carpenter, the son of Joseph and Mary, the Son of God—God incarnate. The depth of His love was shown through His death on a cross, a death He suffered for you and me. He died willingly because it was the only way He could rescue us. Had Jesus not died, it would be impossible for any to enter into eternity and dwell with the Father. Through faith in Jesus Christ, the imperfect man is made perfect in the sight of God. Man is invited into the kingdom of heaven through Jesus' death on the cross.

If you have not opened the door yet by speaking in faith to let Jesus enter (*and I say this with greater depth of heart than anything I have written in this book*), I pray to God that you will. It is by opening the door in faith that a new life you have never known will be opened up. It is a life of hardship and pain at times, but all of that pain and suffering is powerfully outweighed by the deep and loving fellowship of the Father. If you open the door, you will find a life worth living, for it is a life lived in fullness that leads to the gates of eternity.

A Letter to You, the Believer in Jesus Christ

Dear brother/sister,

So you have already, in faith, opened the door to allow Jesus in. Let me first say that I look forward to meeting you on the other side where we will rejoice with the Savior together. One day we will worship hand in hand within the Lord's courts, celebrating the day that we invited Jesus in to our lives. Until then we commune in a world filled with darkness, but one day we will enter into the kingdom of light and stand together filled with joy and heartfelt worship that goes beyond words. We long for this day, but it has not yet come.

Therefore, my dear friend, I turn now to ask you some questions. How will you use this life God has entrusted to you? Will you be someone who chases after the Father? Will you seek to know God better every day, and thereby learn to love and trust Him more and more deeply? Will you allow the knowledge and love of God to fuel your commitment to fellowship with the saints who are also chasing after Him? Will you let the love and truth of God flow through you to your spouse and children, to your parents and siblings, to everyone in your circle of influence? Will you share the love and truth of God with everyone who needs it, each in the way that is appropriate to him or her? And will you die daily to your self—to your self-centered dreams and plans—in order to be fully available for the amazing life God has called you to live?

This is the part where you say, "I will." And I say it with you.

This is the life that we are called to live. A life filled with chasing after the God we love because He first loved us (1 John 4:19). A life for the purpose of sharing the message that saved us from hell and welcomed us into heaven. Never forget that it was pierced hands that reached out to save us and pierced feet that walk by our side. Don't be afraid of suffering similar wounds if it means the chance to save another. In so doing you live and love like Jesus and run hand in hand with Him to the one and only loving and eternal Father.

A Letter to Dad

Dear Dad,

I love you. Without you, this book would have never been written. I never knew what it was to be a man until you yourself became a son who chased the Father. It was the change that I saw in you that inspired me to give God my all. You didn't know if I would follow behind you to the cross where Jesus transforms us wretched men. Rest assured that I have. Thank you for paving a clear and discernable path way to God that I was able to easily follow. I pray that my young sons will now follow behind me as I followed you and see what it means to chase the Father for themselves. I pray this prayer for all men with children. I also pray this prayer for men without children, that they too might help inspire a generation in need of God's transforming power.

There was a time in my life when I felt that I hardly knew you, but now I rejoice that we will have all of eternity to get to know one another. We both know that you are imperfect, but you chase a perfect Father. You have been and continue to be an inspiration to me. I don't know how much time I have left to learn from you in this world, but please know that I am grateful for every minute that I get with you. Spending time with you has helped me to know the truth, speak the truth and live in truth. May we strive to know Jesus Christ more and more until the end of this life. May our relationship bound in Christ be an inspiration to other men. And may those men be an inspiration too.

> With love from your son who seeks to honor you,
> Joshua David Zarzana

In the End

I have heard that the best way to conclude a book is to make the reader feel hopeful in the end. I have hopes, but what I hope for on my own accord really does not mean that much, for I am only one man. But if men would only come together and live one hope in unity, then I think something real significant could happen. What you and I hope for, together, makes all the difference in the world.

And so, I don't want you to feel hopeful in just reading a book. I want you to feel hopeful in something that goes much deeper than that. I want you to feel hopeful that this world still has some good in it worth fighting for, and that perhaps you—*perhaps you*—are meant to fight for that good.

Hopeful…

…that even in despair, God's goodness can burst forth in its time.

…that the decisions you make today, and in all the days that follow, will have an impact on the kingdom of God for the better.

…that you too can be closer to the Father, no matter where you are in life.

…that you also have come to a place where you want to chase God.

…that you will live according to the Spirit and resist the things of the flesh.

…that we will one day be together in eternity, a place where no tear of sadness is welcome, but tears of joy flow in abundance.

…that in the end, we will worship God together.

Hopeful…that you will meet the Savior face to face and hear those long awaited words, "Well done, good and faithful servant" (Matthew 25:23).

So this is where my book ends, and where you choose how the rest of your book will go. I hope that both of our final chapters of life will end up in the same place, in the Father's loving embrace. Yes, my friend, I truly do hope the best for you, but even more than that, so does God. And on that day when you close your eyes for the last time, and embrace the call of death, what is it that you will see when you open your eyes next?

Well, the answer to that question very much depends on you. What will you see?